A STUDY OF

FINANCIAL ANALYSIS OF

LIFE INSURANCE CORPORATION OF INDIA

:: Author ::

Prakash Parmar
(M.Com., B.ed.,NET., M.B.A)

PUBLISHED BY

Hemchandracharya International Publishing House
HQ. At & Po. Chaveli., Ta- Chansma,
Dist- Patan, North Gujarat, India, Asia.
www.iphouseindia.com

First Publication: 10TH FEBRUARY, 2015

Copyright: Author

(c) **Prakash Parmar**

ISBN:- 978-15-08712-20-6

Price: Rs.800/- INDIA

    $ 15 OUTSIDE INDIA

PUBLISHED BY

Hemchandracharya International Publishing House
HQ. At & Po. Chaveli., Ta- Chansma,
Dist- Patan, North Gujarat, India, Asia.
www.iphouseindia.com

INDEX

Sr. No.	Content	Page No.
	Chapters	
1	AN OVERVIEW OF INSURANCE INDUSTRIES	1
2	CONCEPTUAL FRAMEWORK OF FINANCIAL STATEMENT ANALYSIS	50
3	RESEARCH METHODOLOGY	69
4	ANALYSIS OF DATA	81
5	FINDINGS , CONCLUSION AND SUGGESTIONS	118
	BIBLIOGRAPHY	123
	ANNUAL REPORTS OF LIFE INSURANCE COMPANIES OF INDIA	125-126

CHAPTER-1

<u>AN OVERVIEW OF LIFE INSURANCE INDUSTIRES</u>

1.1   INTRODUCTION OF INSURANCE

1.2   BENEFITS OF INSURANCE

1.3   A BRIEF HISTORY OF LIFE INSURANCE

1.4   INTRODUCTION TO INDIAN INUSURANCE INDUSTRY

1.5   INSURANCE REGULATORY DEVELOPMENT AUTHORITY, 1999 (IRDA)

1.6   INSURANCE SECTOR REFORMS

1.7   PRINCIPLES OF LIFE INSURANCE

1.8   INSURANCE AS A SOCIAL SECURITY TOOL

1.9   COMPOSITON OF INSURANCE INDUSTRY

1.10 IMPORTANCE OF INSURANCE IN INDIA

1.11 CALSSIFICATION FO RISK

1.12 MOSTLY ADOPTED KINDS OF INSURANCE

1.13 LIFE INSURANCE DOCUMENTS

1.14 WHAT IS CLAIM?

1.15 ROLE OF INSURANCE IN ECONOMIC DEVELOPMENT IN INDIA

1.16 AN OVERVIEW OF LIFE INSURANCE CORPORATION OF INDIA

1.17 REFERENCES

CHAPTER-I
AN OVERVIEW OF LIFE INSURANCE INDUSTIRES

1.1 INTRODUCTION OF INSURANCE

❖ General Idea

Insurance is a very familiar word for the all but it is not only a word, fundamentally it is a sharing device. Many times natural disasters like Tsunami, Flood, Earthquake, Thunder etc., Prove hazardous to human assets, hence to cope up with this loss large number of person inverts to save themselves from unforeseen calamities. And this contribution of many is used to help the unfortunate who suffered the loss. But there are two condition. First is that the loss should occur as a result of natural or unexpected calamities which beyond our power. Secondly insured person should not make any gains out of insurance.

The business of insurance is concerned with the protection which is provide to the economic values of physical assets such as house, car or shops insurance, But these materialistic facilities are gift for human whose efforts make possible the creation of the assets. In that sense human life is unique source for the production of assets. As time passes the physical assets losses their value but individual becomes more valuable with experiences and skills. Unlike Physical assets, this raises his earning capacity. And this is the starting point or called aim of life insurance is to protect the income of individual and provide financial security to his family, which depends on his income today and after his premature death also.

As we all know this age is a 'capital era' so it is evident for human being that he or she has to secure his or her future financially. For his or her inability for earning money with passing years. one more benefit is that the investment in insurance policy develops the habit of saving. Thus Insurance is too who makes a man self dependent and gives him strength to overcome from any advertises with triumph "Jindgi ke sath Bhi, Jindgi ke baad Bhi"

❖ Definition of Life Insurance

Life Insurance is defined as follows: "Life insurance provides a sum of money if the person who is insured dies whilst the policy is in effect"[1]

❖ Characteristics of the Insurance

- Sharing of risks.
- Co-Operative device
- Evaluation of risks
- Insurance is a plan, which spreads risk and losses of few people among a large number of people.
- The amount of payment depends on the nature of losses incurred.
- The insurance is a plan in which the insured transfers his risk on the insurer.
- The success of insurance business depends on the large number of people insured against similar risk.
- Insurance is a legal contract which is based upon certain principles of insurance which includes utmost good faith, insurable interest, contribution, indemnity, subrogation etc.
- The scope of insurance is much wider and extensive.

❖ Functions of Insurance:[2]

1. Primary Functions:

- **Provide Protection:**

Insurance can not check the happening of the risk, but can provide for the losses of risk.

- **Collective bearing of risk:**

Insurance is a device to share the financial losses of few among many others.

- **Assessment of risk:**

Insurance determines the probable volumes of risk by evaluating various factors that gives rise to risk.

- **Provide certainty:**

Insurance is a device, which helps to change from uncertainty to certainty.

2. Secondary functions:

- **Prevention of losses:**

Insurance cautions businessman and Individuals to adopt suitable device to prevent unfortunate consequences of risk by observing safety instructions.

- **Small capital to cover large risks:**

Insurance relives the businessman from security investment, by paying small amount of insurance against larger risks and uncertainty. And contributes towards developments of larger industries.

3. Other function:

Means of saving and investment.

❖ Classification of Insurance

Insurance business is divided into two broad categories, life and Non life.

Life insurance is concerned with making provision for a specific event happening to the individual, such as death whereas Non-life (general) insurance is more commonly concerned with the provision for a specific event which affects a property, such as fire, flood, theft etc.

❖ Need for life Insurance

The above definition captures the original, basic, intention of life insurance: i.e. to provide for one's family and perhaps others in the event of death, especially premature death. Originally, policies were made to provide for short period of time, covering temporary risk situations, such as sea voyages. As Life insurance became more established, it was found to be a useful tool for following number of situations:

1. Temporary needs/threats

The original purpose of life insurance remains an important element, namely providing for replacement of income on death etc.

2. Regular savings

Providing for one's family and oneself, as a medium to long term exercise(through a series of regular payment of premiums). This has become more relevant in recent times as people seek financial independence from their family.

3. Investment

One has to simply put the building up of savings while safeguarding it from the ravages of inflation. Unlike regular saving products, investment products are traditionally lump sum investments, where the individual makes a one time payment.

4. Retirement

Provisions for one's own later years become increasingly necessary, especially in a changing cultural and social environment. One can buy a suitable insurance policy, which will provide periodical payments in one's old age.

1.2   BENEFITS OF INSURANCE

Insurance is the instrument of security, saving and peace of mind. It provides several benefits by paying a small amount of premium to an insurance company as:

1. It encourages saving and forces thrift.
2. It provided easy settlement and protection against creditors.
3. It helps to achieve the purpose of the life Assured.
4. It can be encased and facilitates borrowing.
5. Tax relief.
6. It is superior for traditional saving vehicles.
7. security against a personal loan, housing loan or other types of loan

8. Provide a protection cover to industries, agriculture, women and child.

9. Provides a piece of mind in case of financial loss.

10.   Safeguards oneself and one's family for future requirements.

(Life insurance is universally acknowledged as a tool to eliminate risk, substitute certainly for uncertainly and ensure timely aid of the family in the unfortunate event of the death of the breadwinner. In other it is the civilized world's partial solution to the problems caused by death.)[3]

In a nutshell, life insurance helps in two ways: premium death, which leaves dependent families to fend for itself and old age without visible means of support.

1.3   BRIEF HISTORY OF LIFE INSURANCE

The business of life insurance In India in its existing from

started in India in the year 1818 with the establishment of Oriental Life Insurance company in Calcutta.

Some of the important milestones in the Life Insurance business in India are:

• **1870:** Bombay Mutual Life Assurance Society, the first Indian life insurance company started its business.

• **1912 :** The Indian Life Assurance Companies Act enacted as the first statue to regulate the life Insurance business.

• **1928:** The Indian Insurance companies Act enacted to enable the government to collect statistical information about both life and Non-life insurance business.

• **1938:** Earlier legislation consolidated and amended to by the Insurance Act with the objective of protecting the interests of the insuring public.

• **1956:** 245 Indian and foreign insurers and provident societies taken over by the central government and Nationalized. L.I.C formed by an Act of parliament, viz. LIC Act, 1956, with a capital contribution of Rs.5 Crore from the government of India.

Life Insurance Corporation Of India was established.

- **1973:** Non life Insurance business of 107 private operators was taken over by the government.

General Insurance Corporation of India and its four subsidiaries were set up in 1973.

- **1999:** Insurance Regulatory and Development Authority bill was passed in parliament in December 1999.

- **2000:** IRDA, independent insurance authority like SEBI established in April 2000.

- Private insurance companies are allowed since September 2000.

Life Insurance is a contract for payment of a sum of money to the person assured(or failing him/her, to the person entitled to receive the same) on the happening of the event insured against.

Usually the insurance contract provides for the payment of amount on the date of maturity or at specified dates at periodic intervals or at unfortunate death if occurs earlier. Obviously, there is a price to be paid for this benefit among other things, the contract also provides for the payment of premiums by the assured. (Life insurance is universally acknowledged as a tool to eliminate risk, substitute certainty for uncertainty an ensure timely aid of the family in the unfortunate event of the death of the breadwinner. In other words, it is the civilized world's partial solution to the problem caused by the death.

1.4 INTRODUCTION TO INDIAN INSURANCE INDUSTRY

The insurance landscape in India is in the process of tremendous change. Closed to foreign competition due to nationalization in 1956, the Indian insurance industry was run by the Government for over 40 years through the Life Insurance Corporation Of India(LIC) and four general Insurance companies that spanned the length and breath of the country. While these companies had done a commendable job in helping the industry grow, the task of making an essential financial product available to the masses gave scope to several other companies, to participate in the arena.

A look at the numbers reveals all. An informal estimate has been made by various experts to assess the existing insurance market in India in terms of premium income. Out of and insurable population of 300 million, 50 million have the capacity to pay a premium of US$300 (Rs.10,500) per year, 100 million have the capacity to pay US$200 (Rs.7,000) per year and 150 million have the capacity to pay US$100(3,500) per year. On the basis the total annual insurance premium would be US$50 billion(Rs.1750bn). The official national Income(GDP) naturally excludes finance available in the parallel economy.

India has an amorphous middle-class of about 300 million people who can afford to buy life, health and disability and pension plan products. Out of this only 20% have insurance and that too covers only 25% of their needs and financial capacity. The remaining 80% have no insurance cover. The life insurance market of India therefore is practically untapped.

India has an enormous middle class that can afford to buy life, health and disability and pension plan products. The low level of penetration of life insurance in India compared to other developed nations can be judged by a comparison of per capita life premium.

India has traditionally been a high savings oriented country – often described as being on par with the thrifty Japan. Insurance sector in the US of A is as big in size as the banking industry there. This gives us an idea of how important the sector is. Insurance sector channeled the savings of the people to long term investments. In India where infrastructure is said to be of critical Importance, this sector will bring the nations own money for the nation. In three years time we would expect the 10% of the population to be under some sort of an insurance cover. This assuming a premium of Rs.5,000 on an average amount to 100 million x Rs.5,000 = Rs.500 bn.

India is the largest democracy in the world having a population more than one billion. It is 5th largest in the world in terms of purchasing power of parity(ppp). India GDP growth rate is over 6% per year on average for the last decade and saving rate is around 26% of GDP.

The insurance sector in India has come to a full circle from being an open competitive market to nationalization and back to a liberalized market again. Tracing the developments in the Indian insurance sector reveals the 360 degree turn witnessed over a period of almost two centuries.

Trough India's Economic development, it becomes the most lucrative insurance markets in the world. Before the year 1999 there were monopoly of state run Life Insurance Corporation Of India and General Insurance of India with Four subsidiaries in general sector. In the wake of reform process and passing Insurance Regulatory Development Act (IRDA) through Indian Insurance was opened for private companies.

1.5 INSURANCE REGULATORY DEVELOPMENT AUTHORITY, 1999 (IRDA)

- **MISSION**

"To protect the interests of the policyholders, to regulate, promote and ensure orderly growth of the insurance industry and for matters connected therewith or incidental thereto"

On the recommendation of Malhotra Committee, an Insurance Regulatory Development Act (IRDA) passed by Indian parliament in 1993. Its main aim is to activate an insurance regulatory apparatus essential for proper monitoring and control of the Insurance industry. Due to this Act several Indian private companies have entered into the

Insurance market, and some companies have joined with foreign partners.

IRDA is a revolutionary piece of legislation. The IRDA was established to regulate, promote & ensure orderly growth of the Life and General Insurance Industry.

The Authority consists of the following Members:

1. A Chairperson
2. Not more than five whole-time members
3. Not more than four Part-time members[10]

- **Functions of IRDA**

1. To exercise all powers and functions of controller of insurance
2. Protection of the interests of the policy holders.
3. To issue, renew, modify, withdraw or suspend certificate of registration.
4. To specify requisite qualifications and training for insurance intermediaries and agents.
5. To promote and regulate professional organizations connected with Insurance.
6. To conduct inspection/ investigation etc.
7. To prescribe method of Insurance Accounting.
8. To regulate investment of funds and margins of solvency.
9. To adjudicate upon disputes.
10. To conduct inspection and audit of insurers, intermediaries and other organizations concerned with insurance.[11]

- **Rights of IRDA**

It has the right to enquire into the affairs of the books and documents of the broker.

It has the right to look into the complaints from clients of the brokers.[12]

- **IRDA Regulations**

In its role to protect policy holder's interests, IRDA stipulates in its regulations relevant to claim settlement that-

In case of death claim, all the requirements should be asked for at one time and not in the piecemeal.

Insurer's decision to accept or repudiate a death claim should be made within 30 days from the date of receipt of claim papers.

If an investigation is necessary, it should be completed within 6 months. In case of delay in settlements of death claim- If the delay is on the part of insurer, interest at 2% over the bank rate would be payable. If delay is due to claimant being not ready to collect the claim amount, rest at the savings bank rate is payable.[13]

1.6 INSURANCE SECTOR REFORMS

In 1993, Malhotra committee, headed by former Finance Secretary and RBI Governor R.N. Malhotra, was formed to evaluate the Indian Insurance Industry and recommend its future directions. The Malhotra committee was set up with the objective of complementing the reforms initiated in the financial sector. The reforms where formed at " Creating a more efficient and competitive financial system suitable for the requirement of the economy keeping in the mind the structural changes currently underway and recognizing that insurance is an important part of the overall financial system where it was necessary to address the need for similar reforms…". In 1994, the committee submitted the report and some of the key recommendations included:

STRUCTURE

1. Government stake in the insurance companies to be brought down to 50%

2. Government should take over the holdings of GIC and its subsidiaries so that these subsidiaries can act as independent corporations.

3. All the insurance companies should be given greater freedom to operate.[14]

COMPETITION

1. Private companies with a minimum paid up capital of Rs.1bn should be allowed to enter the industry.

2. No company should deal in both Life and General Insurance through a single entity.

3. Foreign companies may be allowed to enter the industry in collaboration with the domestic companies.

4. Postal Life Insurance should be allowed to operate in the Rural Market.

5. Only one Statement Level Life Insurance Company should be allowed to operate in each state.

1. The Insurance act should be changed.

2. An Insurance Regulatory body should be set up.

3. Controller of Insurance (Currently a part from the Finance Ministry) should be made independent.[15]

INVESTMENTS

1. Mandatory Investments of LIC life Fund in government securities to be reduced from 75% to 50%.

2. GIC and its subsidiaries are not to hold more than 5% in any company (There current holdings to be brought down to this level over a period of time).

CUSTOMER SERVICE

1. Customer should pay interest on delays in payments beyond 30 days.

2. Insurance companies must be encouraged to set up unit linked pension plans.

3. Computerization of operations and updating of technology to be carried out in the insurance industry.

1.7 PRINCIPLES OF LIFE INSURANCE:

1. Life insurance contracts

A life insurance policy is a contract, in terms of the Indian Contract Act, 1872. A contract is a defined as:

"A contract is an agreement between two or more parties to do or not to do so as to create a legally binding relationship"[16]

A simple contract must have the following essentials:

- Offer and acceptance
- Consideration
- Capacity to contract
- Consensus 'ad idem' (genuine meeting of minds)
- Legality of object or purpose
- Capability of performance
- Intention to create legal relationship

2. Principle of utmost good faith:

- **Definition of utmost Good faith:-**

A positive duty to voluntarily disclose, accurately and fully, all facts material to the risk being proposed, whether requested or not.[17]

- **Material Facts:-**

A fact that would influence the judgment of a prudent insurer in deciding whether to insure a particular risk, or the terms on which to insure it. The declaration made by the proposer, while proposing for insurance, becomes important, as the proposer certifies that the statements given by him are true and that they form the basis of the contract.

- **Disclosure of material facts:-**

The categories of facts that must be declared are the following:

1. Facts, which show that the particular risk represents the greater exposure than normal.

2. External factors, those situations, which make the risk greater than would normally be expected.

3. Any refusal or special term imposed on previous proposals by other life insurers.

4. The existence of other life insurance policies.

5. Full facts relating to the health of the individual taking insurance.

- **Non-Disclosure of Material Facts:-**

There are some circumstances which are material but it is not necessary to disclose. The areas concerned are:

- Facts of law

- Facts of common Knowledge, which every one is supposed to know.

- Facts which a survey would be revealed.

- Facts which could be reasonably discovered , by reference to pervious policies and records available with the insurer.

- **The declaration:**

Proposal forms contain a declaration by the proposer to the effect that all statements and answers furnished by him in the proposal form are true. These statements and declarations shall be the basis of the contract. If any of the statements are false, the contract can be made null and void, by the insurer, and premiums forfeited.

3. Principle of insurable Interest:

- **Definition:-**

"Relationship with the subject matter(a person) which is recognized in law and gives a legal right to insure that person".[18]

- Insurance Interest is a legal pre-requisite for insurance

- The primary interest of a person in the object of insurable such as a house, car, machinery or life which gives him the right to take insurance and so to say, this is insurable interest.

In other words, it is not the house, the car, machinery or life that is insured but it is the pecuniary interest in the object of insurance.

4. **Principle of Indemnity:-**

- Insurance can not be used as means to make profit out of it. The mechanism of Insurance is meant to compensate losses. Simply put, Insurance should not place the insured in a better financial position after loss he enjoyed before the loss. This broadly is the principle of indemnity.

- Compensation on claim can not be more than the extent of insurable interest.

The united nations declaration of Human Rights 1948 provides that "Everyone has a right to a standard of living adequate for the health and wellbeing of himself and his family, including food, clothing, housing and medical care and necessary social services and the right to security in the event of unemployment, sickness, disability, widowhood or the other lack of livelihood in circumstances beyond his control"

In India, social security finds a place in our constitution. Article 41 requires the state , within the limits of its economic capacity and development, to make effective provisions for securing the right work, to education and to provide public assistance in case of unemployment, old age, sickness and disablement and in other cases of undeserved want. Parts of the state's obligations to the poorer sections are met through the mechanism of life Insurance.[19]

Without life insurance, economic condition of the family where the bread winner dies is adversely affected, pushing it down in the society.

Life Insurance in this sense serves a social purpose.

1.8 COMPOSITION OF INSURANCE INDUSTRY

The insurance industry mainly comprises:

- **Insurance carries:**

Insurance carries are large companies that provide insurance and assume the risks covered by the policy.

- **Insurance Agents:**

An insurance agent takes up an agency for selling life insurance policies, while the insurance underwriter reviews insurance applications and decides whether they should be accepted or rejected.

- **Insurance surveyors:**

Insurance surveyors are qualified investigators deputed for the assessment of losses, according to their qualifications and experience.

- **Actuaries:**

An actuaries determines premium rates, studies, mortality trends, constructs mortality tables and lays down underwriting standards.[20]

- **Development officers:**

Development officers in the sector are responsible for the sale of insurance policies in the allotted territorial jurisdiction. They recruit and train the insurance agents.

1.9 IMPOTANCE OF INSURANCE IN INDIA

An insurance sector is of vital importance to every modern economy because it encourages the savings habits; second because it provides a safety net rural and urban enterprises and productive individuals. And it generates long-term funds for infrastructure building.

This characteristics of their business makes insurance companies the biggest sectors in long-gestation infrastructure development projects in all developed and developing countries. This is the most compelling reason why private sector companies which will spread the insurance habit in the societal and consumer interest required in this vital sector of the economy.

With the nation's infrastructure in a state of insurance collapse, India couldn't afford to be lumbered with sub-optimally performing monopoly insurance companies and therefore the passage of the Insurance Regulatory Development Authority.

- **LIBERALIZATION**

    The opening of Insurance sector was a part of the ongoing liberalization in the financial sector of India. With the introduction of the insurance Regulatory and Development Authority (IRDA) bill, the doors were open to the private companies into this sector. The opening up of the sector gave way to the world known names in the industry to enter the Indian market through tie-ups with the eminent business houses. Insurance which was once a quiet business is becoming one of the hottest business today.

- **POST LIBERALIZATION**

    The changing face of financial sector and the entry of several companies in the field of Non-Life, insurance segment are one of the key results of these liberalization efforts. Insurance business by way of generating premium income contributes significantly to the GDP. Despite the fact that the market is vast in India for the insurance business, the coverage is far less compared with the international standards. Estimates show that only 35-40 million, out of a population of 950 million, have come under the umbrella of the Insurance industry.

    The potential of market is so huge that it can grow by 15% to 17% per annum. With the entry of private players, the Indian Insurance Market may finally be able to make deeper penetration in to newer segments and market size will increase rapidly, quality of service will also improve and there will be wide range of products meeting the needs of different customers. The pace for claims settlement is also expected to improve due to increased competition.

    In the general insurance market the need to build trust over time is less important than in the life market because the risk assessment systems and data that are the key to success in the general insurance market are significantly underdeveloped in India even today.

• CHANNEL OF DISTRIBUTION

Till few years back, the only mode of distribution of insurance products was through Agents. While Agents continue to be the predominant distribution channel, today a number of innovative alternative channels are being offered to consumers. A substantial shift in the distribution of Insurance in India is expected. Worldwide, Insurance products. Move along a continuum from pure service products to pure commodity products.

Initially, insurance is seen as a complex product with a high advices and service component. Buyers prefer a face-to-face interaction and place a high premium on brand names and reliability. As products become simpler and awareness increases, they become off-the-shelf, commodity products. Seller move to remote channels such as the telephone or direct mail. Insurance is sold by various intermediaries, not necessarily insurance companies. Some of them are banc assurance, brokers, the internet and direct marketing. Banks and finance companies will emerge as an attractive distribution channel for insurance. This trend will be led by two factors which already apply in other world markets.

First, banking insurance, fund management and other financial services will all form a set of service rather than desperate ones.

Second, banks and finance companies are being driven to increase their profitability and provide maximum value to their customers. Therefore, they are themselves looking for a range of products to distribute. Though it is too early to predict, the wide spread of bank branch network in India could lead to banc assurance emerging as a significant distribution mechanism.

Insurers in India should also explore distribution through Non-financial organization. For example, Insurance for consumer items such as refrigerators can be offered at the point of sale. This piggybacks on an exciting distribution channel and increases the likelihood of insurance sales. Alliances with manufacturers or retailers of consumers with various incentives, of which insurance can be done.

❖ **HIERARCHICAL STRUCTURE INSURANCE COMPANY:**

AN AGENT

↓

**AN AGENCY SALES MANAGER
(UNIT MANAGER OR DEVELOPMENT OFFICER)**

↓

SALES MANAGER/AREA MANAGER

↓

BRANCH MANAGER

↓

REGIONAL MANAGER

↓

CURRENTLY AGENCY SALES HEAD

(source form discussed with life insurance officer head branch at ahmedabad)

1.10 CLASSIFICATION OF RISK

The factor that affects the risk of the individual's life are called "hazards". For the purpose of underwriting, hazards have been classified into the following three categories:

- **Physical hazards**
- **Occupational hazards**

- **Moral hazards**

Physical hazards comprises of:

- Age
- Gender
- Build
- Physical condition
- Physical impairments
- Personal history
- Family history

Occupational hazards comprises of:

- Out of one's job
- Place of work
- Environment and atmosphere at job place

Moral hazards :

- Intention of taking the undue advantage of insurance policy.

1.11 MOSTLY ADOPTED KINDS OF INSURANCE

- **Permanent Life Insurance**

This is the one of that provides for a life time of benefits as long as the premiums are paid as and when they are due. They are beneficial as one can take a loan on the benefits that can be availed on this type of insurance.

- **Term Life Insurance**

It provides protection for a present/limited period of time, and would pay the death benefit only on death happening within the present time. It is considered to be a temporary insurance policy. The premium rates increase at each renewal date. In order to quality for lower premiums, insurers require the insured to provide proof of their insurability.

- **Annuity**

Annuities are practically the same as pensions. They provide regular periodical payments(usually every month) to employees, who have retired. They are paid as long as the recipient it alive. Annuities are called the 'reverse' of life insurance. In annuity contracts, a person agrees to pay to the insurer a specified capital sum in return for a promise from the insurer to make a series of payments to him so long as he lives, while in insurance, the insured pays a series of payments in return for a promise to pay a lump sum on his death.

- **Unit Linked Insurance Plan(ULIP)**

ULIP offers the interesting option of combining the protection and tax advantage of Life Insurance with attractive prospects of investing in securities. The customer decides in which investment fund he wants to invest- money and participate in the performance of selecting funds with all the opportunities and risk that may entail.

Life insurance is universally acknowledged to be an institution which eliminates 'risk' and provides the timely aid to the family in the unfortunate even of death of bread winner.

Life insurance is a written contract between the insured and the insurer that provides for the payment of the insured sum on the date of the maturity of – act or on the unfortunate death of the insured, whichever occurs earlier.

Life insurance is a contract for payment of a sum of money to the person assured (or nominee) on the happening of the event insured against. The contract provides for the payment of premium periodically to the Insurance Company by the assured.

The contract provides for the payment of an amount on the date of maturity or at specified dates at periodic intervals or at unfortunate death, if it occurs earlier.

1.12 LIFE INSURANCE DOCUMENTS

Life insurance documents include the following:

1. Proposal Form

Proposal form usually includes all the personal details of the client as well as the necessary instructions that pertain to the policy. All answers are to be given legibly in words. Strokes of pen or dots or dashes will not be admitted as replies. It contains a declaration at the end of stating that all the statements therein are true in every respect and that if any untrue averment be continued therein, the insurer will be entitled to declare the contract as null and void and forfeit the moneys already paid.

The policy document also makes a reference to this declaration. This declaration makes the principle of utmost good faith operational.

2. First Premium Receipt(FPR)

The FPR is the evidence that the insurance contract has begun. The FPR will state that the proposal for insurance has been accepted and that the premium has been received. It will give the particulars of the policy, such as policy number, date of commencement of risk, date of maturity, date of last payment of premium, premium amount, mode, name and address of the life assured.

3. Policy Document

Policy Document is an evidence of the contract and is not the contract itself. So If policy document is lost duplicate policy can be issued. Policy Document reflects terms of contracts. It contains preamble schedule, attestation, policy conditions and privileges.

4. Policy Clauses

Standardized policy documents would need some modification to bring in line with the actual terms of acceptance. Putting suitable clauses by way of endorsements on the policy can do this.

Some clauses may be imposed at the time of underwriting itself. So as to restrict some of the benefits; some examples are: Endorsement for Extra Premium, Lien clauses, pregnancy clauses, etc. While nomination is done on the policy document itself, assignments or reassignments can be done by way of passing endorsements.

5. Other Documents

During the course of policy, many situations would arise when various documents will have to be obtained.

In case of lost policy, Indemnity Bond may be needed if sum assured is very high.

In case of missing persons, Decree of Court would be needed.

1.13 WHAT IS CLAIM?

Claim is a natural culmination of promise made by the company at the time of entering into the contract. The promise is to pay the stipulated sum assured on the happening of insured contingency. When the contingency takes place, the insurance company can redeem its promise by paying out the claim amount.

There are three major types of claims which are as follows:

1. Maturity Claim

2. Survival Benefits

3. Death Claim

1. Maturity Claim

In this claim under endowment type of policies, the Sum Assured is to be paid when the term of the policy is cover. The date on which the term is complete, is the date of maturity claim. The amount payable on maturity is the Sum Assured, less any debts like loan and interest or outstanding premiums. To this bonuses, If any, would be added it is a with-profit policy.

2. Survival Benefits:

A survival benefits is paid during the currency of the policy, before the date of maturity. The procedure will be similar to payment of maturity claims. Action will be initiated by the insurer and post dated cheque will be sent in advance.

If the life assured dies after the date when the survival benefits was due, but before it is settled, the survival benefit will not be paid to the nominee.

3 Death claim:

The procedures in settling a death claim are more complex than in case of maturity claims. This is mainly because, the facts relating to death have to be studied and the identities of the claimants have to be established.

The death claim action begins with an intimation being received in the insurer's office. The intimation may be sent by the nominee, assignee, a relative of the life assured, the employer, agent or development officer. These intimations may have very little information, other than the policy number, the name of the life assured and the date of death.

The office need not to wait till the intimation of the claim is received. Obituary columns, or newspaper reports in case of accidents or air crashes, may give information and the claim action can be initiated. However, care has to be taken to ensure that the identity of the deceased is established. A name is not enough to establish identity.

The following will be necessary before the death claim is settled:

- Policy Document
- Deeds of assignments/ reassignments
- Proof of age, If age is not admitted.
- Certificate of death
- Legal evidence of title, If the policy is not assigned or nominated.
- Form of discharge executed and witnessed.

In case of rival claimants, court's order would be needed if rival claimant has obtained prohibitory order against the insurer.

In case of early claim, an investigation report from an investigating officer would be needed.

1.14 ROLE OF INSURANCE IN ECONOMIC DEVELOPMENT IN INDIA

For economic development, investments are necessary. Investments are made out of savings. A life insurance company is a major instrument for the mobilization of savings of people, particularly form the middle and lower income groups. This savings are channeled into investments for economic growth. The Insurance Act has strict provisions to ensure that insurance funds are invested in safe avenues, like Government bonds, companies with record of profits and so on.

A Life insurance company's funds are collected by way of premiums. Every premium represents a risk that is covered by that premium. In effect, therefore, these vast amounts represent pooling risks. The funds are collected and held in trust for the benefit of the policyholders. The management of life insurance companies are required to keep this aspect in mind and make all its decisions in ways that benefit the community. This applies also to its investments. That is why successful insurance companies would not be found investing in speculative ventures. Their investments, as in case of the LIC, benefit the society at large.

As on 31-3-2006, the total investments of LIC exceeded Rs.5,20,000 crores, of which nearly Rs.300,000 crores werer directly in Government (both State and Center) related securities, nearly Rs.16,000 crores in the State Electricity Boards, Nearly Rs.22,000 crores in housing loans, Rs.19,000 crores in the power generation(private) sector and Rs.10,000 crores in water supply and sewerage systems. Other Investments included road transport, setting up of industrial estates and directly financing industry. Investments in the corporate sector(Shares, Debentures and term loans) exceeded Rs.30,000 crores. These directly affect the lives of the people and their economic well being.[21]

The LIC is not an exception. All good life insurance companies have huge funds, accumulated through the payments of small amounts of premium of individuals. These funds are invested in ways that contribute substantially for the economic development of the countries in which they do business. The private insurers in India are new and have accumulated funds equal to about One-eighth of the LIC's But even their investments in the various sectors and contributing directly and indirectly to the country's economic development, would be of similar proportions.

1.15 OF INDIA

> **Life Insurance Corporation Of India.**

- **Introduction**

The story of insurance is probably as old as the story of mankind. The same instinct that prompts modern businessmen today to secure themselves against loss and disaster existed in primitive men also. They too sought to avert the evil consequences of fire and flood and loss of life and were willing to make some sort of sacrifice in order to achieve security. Though the concept of insurance is largely a development of the recent past, particularly after the industrial era – past few centuries – yet its beginnings date back almost 6000 years.

Life Insurance in its modern form came to India from England in the year 1818. Oriental Life Insurance Company started by Europeans in Calcutta was the first life insurance company on Indian Soil. All the insurance companies established during that period were brought up with the purpose of looking after the needs of European community and Indian natives were not being insured by these companies. However, later with the efforts of eminent people like Babu Muttylal Seal, the foreign life insurance companies started insuring Indian lives. But Indian lives were being treated as sub-standard lives and heavy extra premiums were being charged on them. Bombay Mutual Life Assurance Society heralded the birth of first Indian life insurance company in the year 1870, and covered Indian lives at normal rates. Starting as Indian enterprise with highly patriotic motives, insurance companies came into existence to carry the message of insurance and social security through insurance to various sectors of society.

Bharat Insurance Company (1896) was also one of such companies inspired by nationalism. The Swadeshi movement of 1905-1907 gave rise to more insurance companies. The United India in Madras, National Indian and National Insurance in Calcutta and the Co-operative Assurance at Lahore were established in 1906. In 1907, Hindustan Co-operative Insurance Company took its birth in one of the rooms of the Jorasanko, house of the great poet Rabindranath Tagore, in Calcutta. The Indian Mercantile, General Assurance and Swadeshi Life (later Bombay Life) were some of the companies established during the same period. Prior to 1912 India had no legislation to regulate insurance business. In the year 1912, the Life Insurance Companies Act, and the Provident Fund Act were passed. The Life Insurance Companies Act, 1912 made it necessary that the premium rate tables and periodical valuations of companies should be certified by an actuary. But the Act discriminated between foreign and Indian companies on many accounts, putting the Indian companies at a disadvantage.

The first two decades of the twentieth century saw lot of growth in insurance business. From 44 companies with total business-in-force as Rs.22.44 crore, it rose to 176 companies with total business-in-force as Rs.298 crore in 1938. During the mushrooming of insurance companies many financially unsound concerns were also floated which failed miserably.

The Insurance Act 1938 was the first legislation governing not only life insurance but also non-life insurance to provide strict state control over insurance business. The demand for nationalization of life insurance industry was made repeatedly in the past but it gathered momentum in 1944 when a bill to amend the Life Insurance Act 1938 was introduced in the Legislative Assembly.

However, it was much later on the 19th of January, 1956, that life insurance in India was nationalized. About 154 Indian insurance companies, 16 non-Indian companies and 75 provident were operating in India at the time of nationalization. Nationalization was accomplished in two stages; initially the management of the companies was taken over by means of an Ordinance, and later, the ownership too by means of a comprehensive bill.

The Parliament of India passed the Life Insurance Corporation Act on the 19th of June 1956, and the Life Insurance Corporation of India was created on 1st September, 1956, with a capital contribution of Rs. 5 crore from the Government of India.

with the objective of spreading life insurance much more widely and in particular to the rural areas with a view to reach all insurable persons in the country, providing them adequate financial cover at a reasonable cost.

- **Logo of the L.I.C$_{23}$**

- **Objective**
- Spread Life Insurance widely and in particular to the rural areas and to the socially and economically backward classes with a view to reaching all insurable persons in the country and providing them adequate financial cover against death at a reasonable cost.

• Maximize mobilization of people's savings by making insurance-linked savings adequately attractive.

• Bear in mind, in the investment of funds, the primary obligation to its policyholders, whose money it holds in trust, without losing sight of the interest of the community as a whole; the funds to be deployed to the best advantage of the investors as well as the community as a whole, keeping in view national priorities and obligations of attractive return.

• Conduct business with utmost economy and with the full realization that the moneys belong to the policyholders.

23. Source from website home page

• Act as trustees of the insured public in their individual and collective capacities.

• Meet the various life insurance needs of the community that would arise in the changing social and economic environment.

• Involve all people working in the Corporation to the best of their capability in furthering the interests of the insured public by providing efficient service with courtesy.

Promote amongst all agents and employees of the Corporation a sense of participation, pride and job satisfaction through discharge of their duties with dedication towards achievement of Corporate Objective.[24]

• **Mission**

"Explore and enhance the quality of life of people through financial security by providing products and services of aspired attributes with competitive returns, and by rendering resources for economic development."[25]

• **Vision**

"A trans-nationally competitive financial conglomerate of significance to societies and Pride of India."[26]

• **Trust**

Every day we wake up to the fact that more than 250 million lives are part of our family called LIC. We are humbled by the magnitude of the responsibility we carry and realize the lives that are associated with us are very valuable indeed.

Though this journey started over five decades ago, we are still conscious of the fact that, while insurance may be a business for us, being part of millions of lives every day for the past 52 years has been a process called TRUST.[27]

- **Members On The Board Of The Corporation**

1. **Shri. T.S. Vijayan**

   (Chairman)

2. **Shri. D.K. Mehrotra**

   (Managing Director - LIC)

3. **Shri. Thomas Mathew T.**

   (Managing Director - LIC)

4. **Shri. A.K. Dasgupta**

   (Managing Director - LIC)

5. **Shri. Ashok Chawla**

   Finance Secretary, Ministry of Finance, Govt. of India)

6. **Shri. R. Gopalan**

   (Secretary, Department of Financial Services, Ministry of Finance, Govt. of India.)

7. **Shri. Yogesh Lohiya**

   (Chairman cum Managing Director, GIC of India

8. **Shri S.Sridhar,**

   Chairmain & Managing Director , Central Bank of India

9. **Dr. Sooranad Rajashekhran, Shri. Monis R. Kidwai**

   Lt. General Arvind Mahajan (Retd.)

   Shri Anup prakash Garg, Shri Sanjay Jain (soruce from website)

- **Operations**
  LIC operate all over India

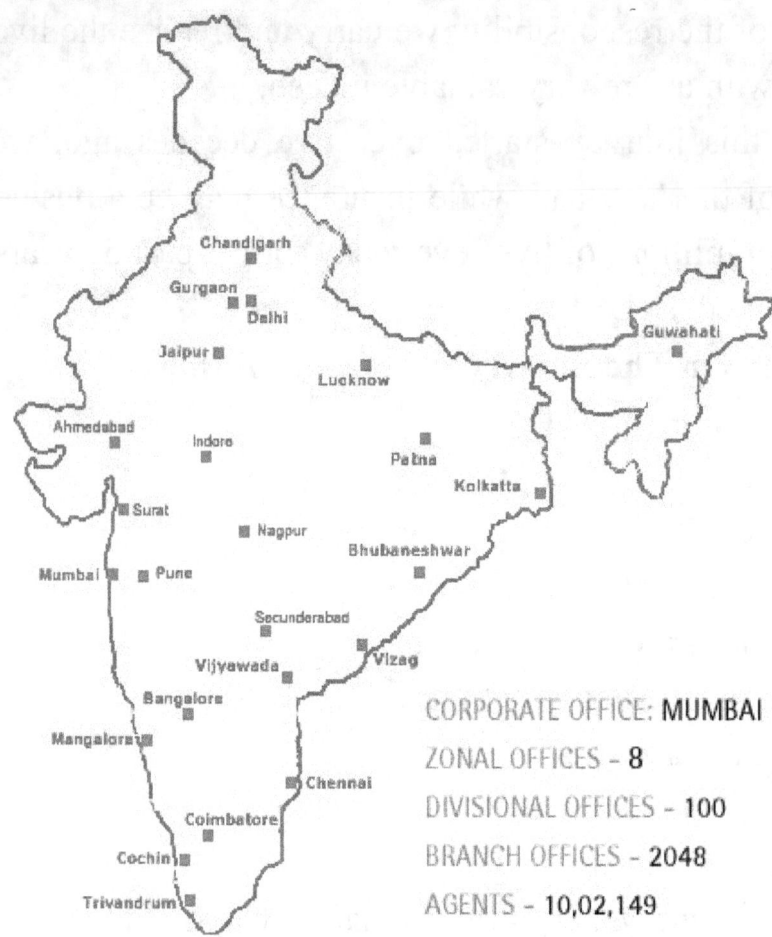

CORPORATE OFFICE: **MUMBAI**

ZONAL OFFICES - **8**

DIVISIONAL OFFICES - **100**

BRANCH OFFICES - **2048**

AGENTS - **10,02,149**

Chart-1 (Source from magazine)

LIC had 5 zonal offices, 33 divisional offices and 212 branch offices, apart from its corporate office in the year 1956. Since life insurance contracts are long term contracts and during the currency of the policy it requires a variety of services need was felt in the later years to expand the operations and place a branch office at each district headquarter. Re-organization of LIC took place and large numbers of new branch offices were opened. As a result of re-organisation servicing functions were transferred to the branches, and branches were made accounting units. It worked wonders with the performance of the corporation. It may be seen that from about 200.00 crores of New Business in 1957 the corporation crossed 1000.00 crores only in the year 1969-70, and it took another 10 years for LIC to cross 2000.00 crore mark of new business. But with re-organisation happening in the early eighties, by 1985-86 LIC had already crossed 7000.00 crore Sum Assured on new policies.[28]

Today LIC functions with 2048 fully computerized branch offices, 109 divisional offices, 8 zonal offices, 992 satallite offices and the Corporate office. LIC's Wide Area Network covers 109 divisional offices and connects all the branches through a Metro Area Network. LIC has tied up with some Banks and Service providers to offer on-line premium collection facility in selected cities. LIC's ECS and ATM premium payment facility is an addition to customer convenience. Apart from on-line Kiosks and IVRS, Info Centres have been commissioned at Mumbai, Ahmedabad, Bangalore, Chennai, Hyderabad, Kolkata, New Delhi, Pune and many other cities. With a vision of providing easy access to its policyholders, LIC has launched its SATELLITE SAMPARK offices. The satellite offices are smaller, leaner and closer to the customer. The digitalized records of the satellite offices will facilitate anywhere servicing and many other conveniences in the future.

LIC continues to be the dominant life insurer even in the liberalized scenario of Indian insurance and is moving fast on a new growth trajectory surpassing its own past records. LIC has issued over one crore policies during the current year. It has crossed the milestone of issuing 1,01,32,955 new policies by 15th Oct, 2005, posting a healthy growth rate of 16.67% over the corresponding period of the previous year.

From then to now, LIC has crossed many milestones and has set unprecedented performance records in various aspects of life insurance business. The same motives which inspired our forefathers to bring insurance into existence in this country inspire us at LIC to take this message of protection to light the lamps of security in as many homes as possible and to help the people in providing security to their families.

- **The Designated Officers at the various offices of the Corporation are:**

At Branch Office

↓

Sr. Branch Manager

At Divisional Office

↓

Marketing Manager

At Zonal Office

↓

Regional Manager (Mktg)

At Central Office

↓

Executive Director (Mktg/IO/CRM)
(source from website)

- **Information technology and LIC**

LIC has been one of the pioneering organizations in India who introduced the leverage of Information Technology in servicing and in their business. Data pertaining to almost 10 crore policies is being held on computers in LIC. We have gone in for relevant and appropriate technology over the years.

1964 saw the introduction of computers in LIC. Unit Record Machines introduced in late 1950's were phased out in 1980's and replaced by Microprocessors based computers in Branch and Divisional Offices for Back Office Computerization. Standardization of Hardware and Software commenced in 1990's. Standard Computer Packages were developed and implemented for Ordinary and Salary Savings Scheme (SSS) Policies.[29]

- **About Insurance Plans**

(source from LIC Product promotional material)

As individuals it is inherent to differ. Each individual's insurance needs and requirements are different from that of the others. LIC's Insurance Plans are policies that talk to you individually and give you the most suitable options that can fit your requirement.

1. Individual Plans

Jeevan Arogya Plan

Jeevan Arogya

Bima Account Plans

Bima Account 1

Bima Account 2

Endowment Plus

Endowment Plus

Children's Plan

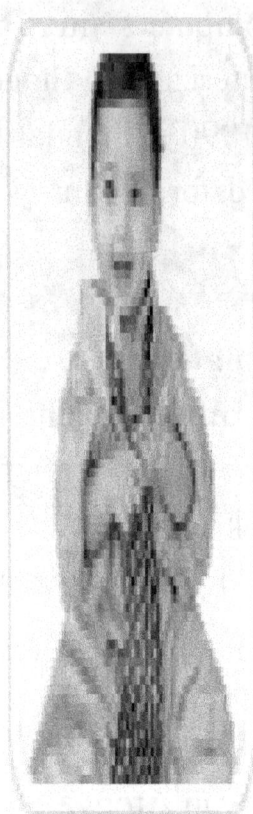

- Jeevan Anurag
- Komal Jeevan

- CDA Endowment Vesting At 21
- Marriage Endowment Or Educational Annuity Plan

- CDA Endowment Vesting At 18

- Jeevan Kishore
- Jeevan Chhaya

- Child Career Plan
- Child Future Plan

Plans For Handicapped Dependents

- Jeevan Aadhar
- Jeevan Vishwas

Endowment Assurance Plans

- The Endowment Assurance Policy
- The Endowment Assurance Policy-Limited Payment
- Jeevan Mitra(Double Cover Endowment Plan)
- Jeevan Mitra(Triple Cover Endowment Plan)
- Jeevan Anand
- New Janaraksha Plan
- Jeevan Amrit

Plans for high worth individuals

- Jeevan Shree-I
- Jeevan Pramukh

Money Back Plans

- The Money Back Policy-20 Years
- The Money Back Policy-25 Years
- Jeevan Surabhi-15 Years
- Jeevan Surabhi-20 Years
- Jeevan Surabhi-25 Years
- Bima Bachat

Joint Life Plan
Jeevan Saathi

Special Money Back Plan for Women
Jeevan Bharati - I

Whole Life Plans
The Whole Life Policy
The Whole Life Policy- Limited Payment
The Whole Life Policy- Single Premium
Jeevan Anand
Jeevan Tarang

Term Assurance Plans
Two Year Temporary Assurance Policy
The Convertible Term Assurance Policy
Anmol Jeevan-I
Amulya Jeevan-I

Decreasing Term Assurance to cover Home Loan Repayment
Mortgage Redemption

2. Unit Plans

Unit plans are investment plans for those who realize the worth of hard-earned money. These plans help you see your savings yield rich benefits and help you save tax even if you don't have consistent income.

Pension Plus

Endowment Plus

3. Pension Plans

Pension Plans are Individual Plans that gaze into your future and foresee financial stability during your old age. These policies are most suited for senior citizens and those planning a secure future, so that you never give up on the best things in life.

Pension Plans

- **Pension Plus**
- **Jeevan Nidhi**
- **Jeevan Akshay-VI**
- **New Jeevan Dhara-I**
- **New Jeevan Suraksha-I**

4. Group Schemes

Group Insurance Scheme is life insurance protection to groups of people. This scheme is ideal for employers, associations, societies etc. and allows you to enjoy group benefits at really low costs.

Group Scheme

- Group Term Insurance Schemes
- **Group Insurance Scheme in Lieu Of EDLI**
- Group Gr-atuity Scheme
- Group Super Annuation Scheme
- **Group Savings Linked Insurance Scheme**
- Group Leave Encashment Scheme
- Group Mortgage Redemption Assurance Scheme
- Group Critical Illness Rider

Social Security Scheme

- JanaShree Bima Yojana (JBY)
- Shiksha Sahayog Yojana
- Aam Admi Bima Yojana

5. Withdrawn Plans

- Jeevan Nischay
- Market Plus I
- Wealth Plus
- Profit Plus
- Jeevan Aastha
- Money Plus-I
- Jeevan Varsha
- Child Fortune Plus
- Fortune plus

- Jeevan saathi Plus
- Health plus
- Samridhi Plus

5. Special Plans

LIC's Special Plans are not plans but opportunities that knock on your door once in a lifetime. These plans are a perfect blend of insurance, investment and a lifetime of happiness!

 **Golden Jubilee Plan**

New Bima Gold

 **Health Plan**

Health Protection Plus

 **Special Plan**

Bima Nivesh 2005

Jeevan Saral

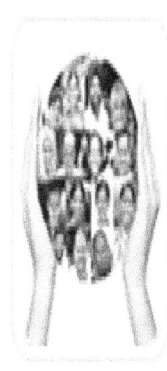 **Micro Insurance Plans**

Jeevan Madhur

Jeevan Mangal

- **Premium Payments**
1. At cash counter – by cash, draft, cheque etc.,
2. Net banking   - through credit card, Debit card etc.
3. alternative channel – A.T.M through

- **Awards**

CNBC Awaaz Consumer awards 2010	**Reader Digest Trusted Brand Insurance category 2010**
OUTLOOK MONEY -- NDTV PROFIT AWARD 2009 in " BEST LIFE INSURER CATEGORY "	World Brand Congress Award

Golden Peacock Innovative
Product / Service Award -
2009

ASIA PACIFIC HRM Congress,
2009 Award for INNOVATIVE
HR PRACTICES

Loyalty Award - 2009

NDTV Profit Business
Leadership Award 2008

INDY's Silver Award for Best
Corporate Film

NASCOM IT USER Award
2008

Business Superbrand India 2009	ASIA BRAND CONGRESS BRAND LEADERSHIP AWARD, 2008
 INDY's Silver Award for Best Corporate Film	
 Reader's Digest Trusted Brand Award, 2009 (Platinum category)	 Golden Peacock Innovative Product / Service Award – 2009

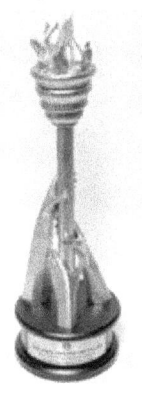

CNBC AWAAZ CONSUMER
AWARD 2009 for
" Most preferred insurance
company "

Brand Equity Most Trusted
Brand 2010 Top in Insurance
Category

INDY's Silver Award for best
Corporate Film

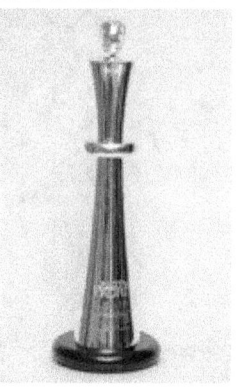

NDTV PROFIT BUSSINESS
LEADERSHIP, AWARDS 2009

INDY's Silver Award for Best
" In-house Magazine "

Pitch Award -" Rank 1 "
India's Top 50 Service Brands

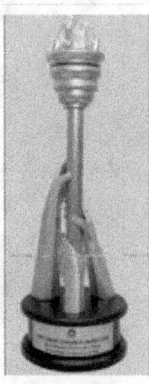

CNBC Awaaz Consumer Awards 2008

Loyalty Award - 2009

Readers Digest Trusted Brand Award 2008 in the Platinum category.

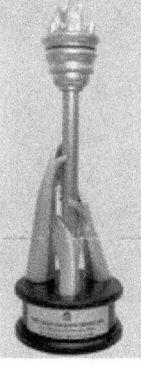

CNBC Awaaz Consumer Awards 2008

NDTV Profit Business Leadership Award 2008

Golden Peacock Award for Excellence in Corporate Governance

Web 18 Genius of the web
awards 2007

NASCOM IT USER Award
2008

Selected Business Superbrand
India 2008

ASIA BRAND CONGRESS
BRAND LEADERSHIP
AWARD, 2008

Loyalty Awards 2008 - Insurance Sector	SKOCH Challengers Award 2008 for Jeevan Madhur

(source from website)

- **Present Status of Life Insurance Corporation of India**

    Existing as a towering **insurance company** for over 50 years, LIC has acquired almost monopoly power in the solicitation and sale of **life insurance policies** in India. In addition to the summary regarding the present stature provided at the beginning, LIC has extended its activities in 12 countries other than India with the objective of catering to the insurance needs of Non Resident Indians.

    The only insurance company belonging to the public sector now has to compete with several other corporate entities of its kind which often are heavyweight Indian as well as **Multinational Life Insurance Brands** in themselves.[30]

The other subsidiary companies under LIC are:

- **Life Insurance Corporation (LIC) of India International** - A joint venture offshore company promoted by **LIC** which commenced its operations in July, 1989 with the objective of offering policies denominated in US $ to NRIs residing in the Gulf.

- **LIC Nepal** - Formed in 2001 in joint venture with Vishal Group of Industries, Nepal.

- **LIC Lanka** - Formed in 2003 in joint venture with Bartlett Group of Companies, Sri Lanka

- **LIC Housing Finance** - Established in 19th June,1989 in Dubai with the objective of providing long term finance for construction of houses or apartments.

- **LIC Housing Finance Limited Care Homes** - A wholly owned subsidiary of **LIC Housing Finance** which builds "Assisted Community Living Centers" for senior citizens.[31]

- ## THE MARKET CHALLENGERS[32]

    There are many challengers in the market.

    Sr. No. Name of the Company

1. Bajaj Allianz life Insurance Company Limited.
2. Birla Sunlife Insurance Company Limited.
3. HDFC Standard Life insurance Company ltd.
4. ICICI Prudential Life Insurance Company Ltd.
5. ING Vysya Life Insurance Company Limited.
6. Max New York Life Insurance Company Limited.
7. Met Life India Insurance Co. Pvt. Ltd.
8. Kotak Mahindra Old Mutual Life Insurance Limited.
9. SBI Life Insurance Co. Ltd
10. Tata AIG Life Insurance Co. Ltd.
11. Reliance Life Insurance Co. Ltd.
12. Aviva Life Insurance Compay India Ltd.
13. Sahara India Life Insurance Company Ltd
14. Sriram Life Insurance Company Ltd.
15. Bharti AXA Life Insurance Company Ltd.
16. Future Generali India Life Insurance Co. Ltd.
17. IDBI Fortis Life Insurance Company Ltd.
18. Canara HSBC Oriental Bank Of Commerce Life Insurance Co. Ltd.
19. AEGON Religare Life Insurance Company Limited.
20. DLF PramErica Life Insurance Company Ltd.
21. Star Union Dai-ichi Life Insurance

1.16 REFERENCES

1. IC-33 Life Insurance (New syllabus)

    S. Balachandran

    Insurance Institute Of India

2. Life insurance Practicies

      Himalaya Publication, New Delhi.

3. Magazine/News paper

    1.   The Tmes Of India

    2.   Life Insurance In India – New Delhi

2. website

    1.   http:// www.google.com //

    2.   http://www.lic.com//

    3.   http://www.irda.com//

Chapter 2
CONCEPTUAL FRAMWORK OF FINANCIAL STATEMENTS
ANALYSIS

2.1 MEANING OF FINANCIAL STATEMENTS

2.2 CONCEPTS FO FINANCIAL STATEMENTS

2.3 OBJECTIVES OF FINANCIAL STATEMENTS

2.4 TYPES OF FINANCIAL STATEMENTS

2.5 IMPORTANCEOF FINANCIAL STATEMENTS

2.6 USERS OF FINANCIAL STATEMENTS

2.7 LIMITATIONS OF FINANCIAL STATEMENTS

2.8 CONCEPTS OF FINANCIAL STATEMENTS

2.9 TYPES OF FINANCIAL STATEMENTS

2.10 NEED AND AIMS OF FINANCIAL STATEMENTS

2.11 TOOLS AND TECHNIQUES OF FINANCIAL STATEMENTS

2.12 REFERENCES

2.1 MEANING OF FINANCIAL STATEMENTS

Financial Statement generally consists of three basic statements the income statement, the profits and loss account and the Balance sheet. The statement of the earnings and sources and uses o funds statements financial statement taken to gather, give the financial statement, taken to gather, give accounting picture at the first operation and financial position. The package of finance statement includes such schedules as the relating to fixed assets, long term investment long tem debts. Accrued liabilities. Cost of goods manufactured, selling expresses and administrative and general expenses. There schedules mainly supplement the information contained in the financial statement and are considered essential for the purpose at analysis. In addition, explanatory from notes are also given as an integral past at financial statements when the information given in the financial statement and schedules are inadequate.   The inventory valuation and at depreciation, description at contingent liabilities etc.

2.2 CONCEPTS FO FINANCIAL STATEMENTS

One at the most important functions at the accounting process is to accumulate and report historical accounting information the most prominent examples at such reports are the general purpose financial statement showing an organizational financial position and results of it's operation. These financial statements are the end results at its operations. These financial statements are the end result at the process at financial accounting.

In the words at Hampton, "A financial statement is an organized collection at data organized according to logical and insistent accounting procedure"[1] There fore, all the statements and accounting reports which the accountants prepare the end at t period for a business enterprise may be taken as financial statements. But the principal financial statements, But the principal financial statements are the 'balance sheet' and the profit and loss account.

In the word at Howard and Upton" although any formal financial statements expressed in only values meant be thought at as financial statements, The term has come to be limited sheet' and the ' profit and loss statements' The balance sheet states the assets, liabilities and capital of the business profit and loss statements shows the results of reparations achieved during a certain period These financial statement may be of various types, but according to the financial statement may be broadly classified in the following manner:

1. The audited statement
2. The interim statement
3. The unedited year-end statement
4. The "estimated" statement

Accounting which is the process at evolution has there phases: (1) the recording at transaction in the books at original entry. (2) The classification at these rams action in ledges and (3) the summarization of the records. The construction at the financial statement is a part at the third phase at accounting techniques. Thus, financial statements summarized periodical reports at financial and operating data accumulated by an enterprise in its books at accounts financial statements are periodical statement and the period for which they relate is knows as accounting period, usually at one years' duration.

2.3 OBJECTIVES OF FINANCIAL STATEMENTS

The accounting principles board of America mentions the objectives of financial statement as follows:

1. To provide reliable financial information about economic resources and obligations at a business enterprise

2. To Provide reliable information about in net resources at on enterprise that results form its activates

3. To provide financial information that assist in estimating the earning potentials at a business.

4. To provide others needed information about changers in economic resources of obligation

5. To disclose, to the extent possible, others information related to the financial statements that is relevant to the needs at the users at these statements.

The above objectives and to suit the needs at the varied users, the accountant entrusted with the task of compiling and presenting financial statements must follow a set at guidelines to ensure consistency, completeness and fairness of the statements. This guideline is called statement. These guidelines use called "generally accepted accounting principles" in absence of these' generally accepted accounting principles' The statement prepared may be un-understandable and misleading for the various groups at users.

2.4 TYPES OF FINANCIAL STATEMENTS

The time is gone when leaflet or dance card' type of annual report ands considered sufficient as a folders in which chairman and accountant' blessed' condensed financial summaries. But in the present the annual reports contain financial statements and the explanation at the various financial results.

These are two major financial statements which are vital to financial analysis and financial management i.e. profit and loss account and balance sheet. These statements contain various information's often needed by various persons intersected in the enterprise such as shareholder, government, debenture holder, management ET. They convey the finical condition and results operation of a enterprise for a given period and of a given data. In the annual report, to gather with these tow statement, these may be statements schedules of retained earnings, stockholders, equity statement or capital surplus fund, cash flow statement etc. Acco9unting is a language of 'finance' or 'monetary' A lay man who reds these statements is not able to understand the terminology uses in these statement.

A. **Balance Sheet:**

The balance sheet is a statement at asset and liabilities of a rim or what it own and what it owes, as on a given data. In a bale sheet, the assets and liabilities are equal to each others in the word or pile, white and loosen "A balance sheet is so called because its tow sides must always bale, the sum of the assets shown on the bale sheet must equal liabilities plus owner equality. According to block and first," The balance sheet indicates what the firm owns, and how these assets are financed in the form of liabilities or ownership interest"$_2$

The balance sheet is also known attempt of financial condition, 'statement of financial position, stamen of Assets and liabilities,' statement of assets, liabilities and capital,' statement of word and 'financial stamen' it is an instantaneous photograph of assets, liabilities and net girth It is a financial positions of a business of a specified moment of time it represents all assets owned by the business at a particulars moment of the and the claims at the omens and out spiders against those asset at that the financial condition at the business at that time.

B. **Income Statements.**

The income statement, usually designated as profit and loss accounts for the relevant financial users, shows the net profit as net loss. Resulting from the operations at business during a special field period at time. The items appearing in it use in the nature of 'revenue'.

In the words at Walgenbach, Dietrich and Hanson, "To show the results at operations for a period, an income statement is prepared, which lists the revenues and expenses and presents the resulting net income amount.[3] Fouler defines income statement as' the mathematical interpretation at the policies, experience, knowledge, foresight. And aggressiveness of the management at a business enterprise.[4]

The income statement summarizes the changes that have taken place since the data at preceding bale sheet and that have affected the owner's share in the business either by gain or loss. It is a performance report seconding the changes in income. expenses, profit and loss as a result at business operations during the year between to balance sheet dates.

According to Guthmann, "The balance sheet might be described as financial cross sections taken at certain intervals and earnings statements as condensed history at the growth at decay between the cross sections.[5]

C. Statement at Retained Earnings.

The Statement at retained earrings indicates the magnitude and causes net changes in retained earnings at a enterprise due to year's activities the defined by walgenbhach and Dietrich "a retained earnings statement is an analysis at the restrained earrings accounts for the accounting period is usually presented with the others corporate financial statement.[6] The stained earnings shown in the statement at retained earrings are retained by the enterprise primarily to expand business,

D. Statement at changer in financial position

The statement at changer in financial position is a logical adjunct to the bale sheet and income statement the according to grant" the statement of changes in financial position is most commonly used to indicate changes during the year in the companies' working capitol position'. The statement of changer in financial position' the stamen at changer in financial position indicate both the source and application of working capital. The statement may emphasize any at the following aspect relating to change in financial position at the business.

1. Changes in the firm's working capital
2. Change in the firm's cash position.
3. Change in the firm's total finical position

2.5   IMPORTANCE OF FINANCIAL STATEMENTS

The importance and usefulness at financial statements, from the point of view at various interested parties, are as follows

A. <u>Management:</u>

Financial statements are at much greeted here to management in understanding the progress, position and prospects at business. Using analogy it can be said that financial statements serve the business management as gouger and charter serve the engineer. Financial statement, management can either plan nor fulfill easily the functions of operation and control.

B. <u>Investors:</u>

Financial statements are salsa significant for investor both present and prospective the investor look to the financial position at business concern from a different angle. Investors are interested in two things firstly; they can't to invest in such situation where the feel the niacin structure at a company is sound. Secondly, the want to invest only in such concern whose future is bright. Investor gives first attention to the profits after taxes in the privet and loss accounts.

C. <u>Bankers:</u>

A bankers is primarily cone rend with the ability at paying current debts mad the Current operation results he wants not nobly the payment at advance but he also wants that such advance should be repaid at proper time also.

D. Government:

Central and state Governments and local authorities are also interested in published financial statements in order to assess their revenues through various taxes to regulate capital issue and public utility equates.

E. Trade Creditors:

From the credited point at view the financial statements act as magic eye highlighting the credit worthiness, i.e., assurance whiter the company will honor obligations as and when thy nature.

F. Labor unions:

From Social solstice pint at view in the present time, the labor unions may know id the labor is getting its fair share at business earnings.

G. Public:

Financial statements are also valuable to the public who are interested in prospects at a concern, in one why or the other it is the sureties at the enterprise alone that are bought and sold on stock exchanges and the public is interested, mostly in their financial standing.

H. Research Scholars:

The financial analysts and research workers are interested in published financial statements for guiding management or for establishing certain principles. And management and offer constructive.

2.6 USERS OF FINANCIAL STATEMENTS

Different classes of people are interested in the financial statement analysis with a view to assessing the economic and financial position of any business or industry in terms at profitable liquidity as solvency.

1. Share holders:

Divorce between ownership and management and broad-based owner at capital due to dispersal at share holding have made share holders take more interest in the financial statement.

2. Debenture holders:

The debenture holder is interested in the short-term as well as the long-term solvency position at company. They have to get their interned payments periodically and at the end the return at the principle amount.

3. Creditors:

Potential suppliers at and material and others going business with the company are interested the liquidity position at the company.

4. Important customers:

Who want to make long standing contact with the company age interested in its financial strength?

5. Employees and Trade unions:

Are interested in the profitability position at the company

6. Government Departments:

Dealing with the industry in which the company is engaged are interested in the financial information relating to the company.

7. SEBI and Stock Exchange:

Are interested in the prospects and performance at listed companies with a view to protecting the interests of investors.

8. Financial institutions and commercial Banks:

These financial institutions are interested in the solvency-short-term as well as long – term and profitability position at the company.

2.7 LIMITATIONS OF FINANCIAL STATEMENTS

The nature at figures which are exported and the any in which they are repotted tend to give the impression to the Spades that financial statements are precise east and final. Financial statements are not from limitations.

1. Balance sheet reveals the facial position at a firm an a particulars day usually at the end at accounting year.

2. Financial statements reflect the seconded facts and figures these are not useful for control purpose.

3. Valuation at inventories, method depreciation, treatment at expend as capital or revenue etc., are based upon personal sidemen.

4. These contain some estimated and such as provision for doubtful debts act.

5. By following money measurements concept ' non- monetary events are not disclosed

6. By following cost concept. Hardest values fixed assets are not shown. Fixed assets are shown at cost lees depreciation.

7. The financial statements do not keep pace with changing price levels.

8. Balance sheet shows the deeded expenses such as preliminary expenses. These are not really assets.

. Many a times, consistency is not followed and hence the profitability is not comparable from years to year. Debt-equity ratio as prescribed by the controller at capital issue is not mentioned in the financial statements.

2.8 CONCEPTS OF FINANCIAL STATEMENTS

Financial Analysis is the analysis of financial statement, viz. Balance sheet and profit and loss account amide at diagnosing the profitability and financial addition business concern satisfactory diagnosis can resell be made in the basis at information which are included financial statements alone because are dumb.

Information contained in balance sheet and profit and loss account often in the form at raw data than as information useful for making. The process of converting the raw data contained in the financial statement analysis.

Profit and loss account is a dynamic statement which shows income expenses between two bale sheets likewise balance sheet is a 'static' statement that shows the financial position on a certain data. Is instantaneous photograph at the and liabilities at an enterprise particular unit at time.

Financial analysis is a process of synthesis and intellectual activity it is a techniques at X- raying the financial position as well as the progress at a company. An analysis at both these statements gives a comprehensive understanding at business operations and their impact at the financial health it the business operations results in profits the toil investments is enhanced bringing prosperity to shareholders, increase in goodwill and strengthening at credit.

2.9 TYPES OF FINANCIAL STATEMENTS

Financial analysis can be classified into different categorizes depending upon.

(A)   On the basis of material used

(B)   The modus operandi at analysis

(A)   On the basis of material used

According to this basis, financial analysis can be at two types.

External analysis:

This analysis is done by those who are outsiders for the business the term outsiders includes investors, credit agencies, government agencies and other creditors who have no access to the internal seconds at the company. The position of these analysis's for increased governmental control over companies and governmental regulations disclosure at information by the companies at financial statements.

2. **Internal analysis:**

This analysis is done by personas that have access to the books of account and other information related to the business. The analysis is done depending upon the objective to be achieved thorough this analysis.

(B) On the basis at modus operandi:[7]

According to, financial analysis can also be at two types.

(1) Horizontal Analysis:

In case at this types at analysis, financial statements for a numbers of years, are seriated and analyzed. The current year's figures are compassed with the standard or base year the analysis statement an analysis gives the management considerable insight into levels and areas of strength and weakness.

(2) Vertical Analysis:

In case at this type of analysis a study is made at the quantitative relationship at the various items in the finical statements in a particular data such an analysis is useful in comparing the performance at several companies in the same group, or divisions or departments in the same company since this analysis depends on the data for cone period, this is not very conducive to proper analysis at the company's financial position

2.10 NEED AND AIMS OF FINANCIAL STATEMENTS

Analysis at financial statements is an effort to find answers to a varsity at practical and important questions such as prospects for future earnings, ability to pay interest, debt maturities-both current as well as long-term and profitability at a sound dividend pokey, etc. The main importance at the strengths and weakness at a business enterprise at financial statement i.e., Balance sheet and profit and loss account

Need for management:

(I) Measuring the success or the failure at the operation as a whole,

(i) Making sound decisions seating to all the phase at operations.

(ii)   Controlling operations and,

(iii)   Efficiency at departments and process.

Need for outside parties:

(i)   Creditors use analysis as a basis for granting credit.

(ii)   Investors use it is come to a decision at buying, selling or holding shares in a company and

(iii)   Government uses it for purposes at regulations and administration.

Aims:

The Main aims at financial analysis are listed as follows:

(i) To judge the financial health at the undertaking or management, creditors and bankers.

(ii)   To judge the earnings performance at the company and facility with which dividends can be paid from out at earned profits.

(iii)   In case at institutional interstaters the analysis is carried cover a long period with a view to identifying companies making growth potential and a sound financial base.

(iv)   To judge the ability at the company to away the principal and interest, arrangements for amortization at debt and the security available for the loans extended

(v)   To judge the solvency at the undertaking, the trade creditors are mainly interested in assessing the liquidity positing for which they look into the following.

(a) Whether the current assets are sufficient to pay at the current liabilities,

(b)   The proposition liquid assets to current assets.

To business prospects with reentrance to the future growth and earning.

2.11 TOOLS AND TECHNIQUES OF FINANCIAL STATEMENTS

There are many techniques which may be used for analyzing the financial statements. These techniques may be classified as follows.

(A) Accounting Techniques:

Accounting techniques okra tool which may used for financial analysis are many such as ratio analysis, common size statement analysis, trend analysis, comparative statement analysis, value added analysis etc. The users pick up the techniques to suit their seamier. Meats and also on the basis data available to them. The accounting techniques which are proposed to be used for the analysis of financial statements.

(1) Ratio Analysis:

The evaluate the financial condition and performance of an enterprise the financial analyst needs certain under sticks cone at such rustics frequently used is a ratio or index, seating two pieces at financial data to each others. Ratios, as a tool at financial management, can be expressed as (a) percentage, (b) fraction, and (c) a stated comparison between numbers

According to batty, "The term "accounting ratios is used to describe significant relationship which exist between figures shown an s island sheet, in a profit and loss account, in a budgetary control, system, or in any other past at the accounting organization"[8]

Financial ratios can be divided into certain categories on the basis at the items which are used for ratios. Four types at financial ratios are commonly used

1.   Liquidity ratios,
2.   Profitability ratios,
3.   Activity ratios, and Leverage ratios

(2) Common-size statement:

The common-size statements are know as 'component percentage statements or know as' component percentage statements or vertical statements. In this technique, the total assets or liabilities and the figure or net sales are taken equal to one hundred and the percentages at individual items are calculated liar wise.

In the common-size income statement, the net sales are assumed to be 100%and other items are expressed, as a percentage at sales. Similarly in the common-size balance sheet the total assets as total liabilities are assumed to be 100% and other items at assets and liabilities are expressed as a percentage at this total

(3) Comparative statement Analysis:

Comparison at financial statements for two or more years is another's techniques used in analyzing data comparative financial statements are statements at financial position at a business so designed as o position at a business so singe as to provide time perspective to the consideration at various elements at financial positing embodied in such statements for this purpose the balance sheet and profit and loss the balance sheet and profit and loss account are prepared in comparative form, comparative statements may be made to show.

- Absolute data (rupee amount or money values,)
- Increase or decrease in absolute values data in terms at money values, and
- Increase or decrease in absolute data in terms at percentages.

(1) Trend Analysis:

Trend analyses , so easy to understand the changes in an items or a group of items over a period of time and to draw conclusion squaring the changes in data for this purpose, a base year is chosen and the amount at that time seating to the base year is taken equal to one hundred and index numbers are to one hundred and index numbers are calculated for other years based on the amounts at that item in those years it is a dynamic method at analysis showing the changes over a period of time for props trend analysis, the trend shod be studied at least over a period at not less tam fovea ears/ This method at analysis indicates the directing in which a concern is gaveling and up9on this basis for future can be made.

(2) **Value added analysis:**

The value added technique to judge the efficiency at an enterprise is at its infancy in India it indicates the net value or wealth created by the manufactures during a specific period. No enterprise can survive as grow, if it fails to generate wealth. An enterprise can survive or grow, it is fails to generate wealth an enterprise may exist without making profit but cannot survive without adding value. The enterprise, not making profit, shall become sill but not adding value may cause its death over a period at time thus the value added is basis and board thus the value added is basic and board measure at judging the performance at an enterprise.

(3) **Funds flow analysis:**

Funds flow analysis has become an important tool in the analytical kit at financial analysis, credit granting institutions and financial managers. This is because the balance sheet at a business reveals its financial status at a particular point at time. However, a financial analyst must know the purpose for which the loan ands utilized and the source from which it was obtained. This will help him in making a better estimate about the company financial position and policies.

Funds flow analysis reveals. The changes in working capital position. Ti about the sources from which the working capital was obtained and the purposes for which it was used. It brings out in open the changes which have taken place behind the balance sheet. Working capital being the life-blood at the business, such an analysis is extremely useful. The technique and the procedure involved in funds flow analysis has been discussed in detail later in the book.

(4) Cash flow Analysis:

A cash flow analysis is another important technique at financial analysis it involves preparation at cash flow statement for identifying sources and application at cash flow statement may be prepared on the basis at actual estimated data in the latter case, it is termed as ' projected cash flow statement', which is synonymous with the term 'cash budget'.

(B) Statistical Techniques:

Use at statistical techniques has become a normal phenomenon in any type at analysis. The statistical techniques, which are proposed to be used in financial statement analysis.

(1) Measures of central tendency:

The measures at central tendency occupy in import anent place in the techniques at statement analysis because many other techniques statistical analysis depend upon this measure.

There are five measure at central tendency (I) arithmetic mean (ii) median (iii) mode (IV) geometric mean (v) harmonic mean.

(2) Measures of dispersion:

There are four common measures at dispersion. Sense quartile deviation, average deviation standard deviation. The measures at dispersion, which are expressed in teeters at the original units at a series, use terms as 'absolute measure' relative measures at dispersion are obtained as rations or percentages known as 'co-efficient' with are pure numbers indecent measurement.

(3) Correlating and reassessing Analysis:

Correlating analysis is a technique sued to test the associating between two sets at paired data while sea session analysis is a techniques to test the functional relationships between two sets at paused data. Reassessing analysis, on the other hand, hypothesizes a particular direction at the relationship with sea session one variable is determined by the others.

(4) Analysis at time series:

The time series is an arrangement at statistical data in accordance with the time at its occurrence. The variation at time series is usually broken down into four component elements; secure trend, seasonal, variation, cyclical variation and stardom or irregular influences.

(5) Analysis at variance:

The analysis at variance. One at the most important tools at statistical analysis, has been developed specially to test the hypothesis whether the means at several samples have significant differences or not in the words at Levin, 'analysis at variance is the test for the significance at the difference between moor than two sample means"[10]

(6) Chi-square Test:

The chi-square test (X) is one at the simplest and most widely used non-parametric test in statistic. According to sesame d. braves man" the chi-square distribution is a continuous probability distribution which has the value zero at its lower limit and extraction negative value chi-square is impossible.[11]

(7) Kraal Wallis one way analysis at variance test:

According to jams v. bravely "this test in the sank randomization analyze at the observation randomization test" William j. Stevenson states, it is a one way analysis at variance test that employs ranks rather than actual measurements, and its assumptions concerning data use selectively weak"[12]

(8) Index Numbers :

According to croton and crowned' index numbers are devices for measuring differences in maqunitude at a group at seated variables"[13] While as per , Morris homburg ' in its simplest form an index number is nothing more than a relative number, or a ' sedative' which expresses the relationship between tow figures, where one at the figures is used as a base"[14]

(9) Diagrammatic and graphic presentation of data:

Diagrams and graphs are visual aids, which give a bird's eye view at a given set at numerical data. They present the data in simple secondly comprehensible and intelligible form graphic presentation at statistical data given a pictorial effect to what would otherwise be just a mass at figures diagrams and graphs depict made information than the data shown in the table.

(10) Mathematical techniques :

The use at various mathematical techniques is also made frequently for financial analysis. The mathematical tools generally applied are- programmed evaluation and review techniques (PERT), critical path method (CPM), linear programming etc. These techniques could not be applied in present study for want at necessary data.

CHAPTER -3
RESEARCH METHODOLOGY

3.1 INTRODUCTION

3.2 THE TITLE OF THE PROBLEM

3.3 PERIOD OF STUDY

3.4 REVIEW OF LITERATURE

3.5 DATA COLLECTION

3.6 OBJECTIVES OF STUDY

3.7 HYPOTHESIS OF THE SUTDY

3.8 TOOLS & TECHNIQUES USED

3.9 CHAPTER PLAN

3.10 LIMITATIONS AT STUDY

3.11 REFERENCES

3.1 Introduction:

The Life insurance industry selected for the present study on account of number of important factors. The Life insurance industry has been playing vital role in the development of the economy of India. Life insurance industry is backbone of every economy. Life insurance industry is one of the most biggest industry in all over the world. Last decades Life insurance industry achieves study growth by attractive regular flow investment and make strong industry.

Generally, Industries raises their funds by various sources like equity share, capital preference share capital, debentures, bonds, deposits etc. It is the most important and crucial problem for every industry to determine the financial requirements. Which are the sources of funds? How to raise funds at minimum costs?

An investor is interested in information regarding the exact financial position of the business, its earning capacity, the present position with regard to profitability and future possibilities. He has only the published accounts of the company before him which would enable him to take any decision with respect to investing his money.

The published accounts contain Revenue Account, P & L Accounts and Balance sheet. The earning capacity and past results could be ascertained from the P & L Accounts and the idea about financial positions can be had from the balance sheets.

However actual conclusion can not be drawn from the mass figures included in the financial statements. So the financial analysis of life insurance companies must be necessary.

3.2 The title of the problem:

So far we take, The title at the problem selected for this study is **"A STUDY OF FINANCIAL ANALYSIS OF LIFE INSURANCE CORPORATION OF INDIA."**

3.3   Period of Study:

For this study we have selected Life Insurance Corporation Of India. The study was based on secondary data. The data relating to the financial statements analysis at the a published annual reports collected data selected Life insurance Corporation of India for the year 2006 to 2010. the secondary data wherever needed opinions journals, magazines, newspapers, accounting, literature on insurance industries have been used in the study for the purpose at analysis at balance sheet and profit and loss account the figures taken from annual reports.

3.4 Review of literature:

1. Prof. S.J.Parmar has also analyzed the profitability and liquidity aspects at cement industries in his research under the title of " profitability analysis at cement indiausries in Gujarat state"

2. Shri N.p Agrwal in this study at financial statements at Indian aluminum industries were analyzed for th title at " analysis at financial statements"

3. The dissertation of kacha geeta on analysis of financial statements of two wheeler industries has attempted to study profitability and liquidity of selected companies using various ratios.

4. **Title**   :-   "A Report On Budgetory control and
                                   Ratio Analysis At "Welspun India Ltd"."

   Researcher   :-   M.S Doliy Mehta

   Year   :-   2009-2011

   Degree   :-   M.B.A

   University   :-   k.s.k.v kachchh University

   Objective   :-   effective Information and knowledge
                                   About finance and management.

   Universe   :-   Indian Textile Industry

   Sampling   :-   Welspun Anjar Group

   Research Method :-   Ratio Analysis and t-test is used.

Conclusion :-

* Within minimum regulation and supportive government policies there are large number of opportunities that the present textile industry is providing.

* The added advantages of cheap domestic labour and demand in foreign markets are all paths towards profitability.

* In ratio analysis like net profit ratio, Inventory turn over ratio, Proprietory ratio suggest that WIL has used borrowed funds more, so the WIL's earning can be increased. So it represents very good financial position of the company. In debtors turn over ratio, the collection of the credit sale is made 11.81 times. So it's very nice

5. **Title**   :-" Ratio Analysis of the Bhuj commercial
                       Co-Operative Bank Ltd. Bhuj kachchh".

Researcher	:-	Meera Palan
Year	:-	2009-2011
Degree	:-	M.B.A
University	:-	k.s.k.v kachchh University
Objective	:-	The present study has been undertaken With following objectives:

* To study the growth and development of BCCB.

* To study the trends in finance and analyze various elements in financial analysis.

* To evaluate the financial position of BCCB.

* To calculate and estimate the important financial ratios as a part of financial analysis in BCCB.

* To offer suggestions to improve financial position of the bank.

* To study the financial strength and weakness of the BCCB.

Universe   :-   Banking Industry

Sampling :- BCCB Bhuj, kachchh
Research Method:- Ratio analysis and t-test used
Conclusion :-

• Results of ratio analysis show that the BCCB's performance is quite good but some more efforts are required for the financial operation.

• According to my opinion and observation I felt that the future of this bank is very bright.

• At last I can say that the BCCB is developing one with for its continues progress for present and future.

6. **Title** :-" Financial statement Analysis of the Bhuj commercial Co-operative bank Ltd. Bhuj"
   Researcher :- Krishna.M Narela
   Year :- 2009-2011
   Degree :- M.B.A
   University :- k.s.k.v kachchh University
   Objective :-

• The role objective of the project is to help the management of the organization in decision making, regarding the subject matter.

• Calculation of financial statement and ration is only the clerical task whereas the interpretation of its needs immense skill, intelligence and foresightedness.

• One of the easiest and most popular ways of evaluating performance of the organization is to compare its present ratios with the past ones called comparison and through development action plan.

   Universe :- Banking Industry
   Sampling :- BCCB Bhuj, kachchh
   Research Method :- Financial statement analysis and

t-test used.

Conclusion :-

- If properly analyzed and interprets, financial statement can provide valuable insight into a firm's performance.

- According to my opinion and observation I felt that the future of this bank is very bright.

- At last I can say that the BCCB is developing one with for its continues progress for present and future.

7. **Title** :- " A study of financial analysis of Reliance Industries limited"

Researcher	:-	Lalit. M Vaniya
Year	:-	March - 2008
Degree	:-	Master Of Philosophy in commerce
University	:-	Saurashtra University, Rajkot
Objective	:-	The main objective at the study.

- To understand financial analysis and it's conceptual framework

- To evaluate the financial analysis with financial statements

- To textile units at reliance industries limited

Universe	:-	Reliance Industry
Sampling	:-	Reliance textile industries
Research Method :-		Financial statement analysis and t-test used.

Conclusion :-

- It can be maintained that the position regarding the net margin is better than that at the operating profit margin at reliance industries limited.

- The total assets turnover ratio which shows the firms ability of generating sales. From all the financial resources.

Committed to the firm, have increased during the period under review, except in the year 2003 in case at both the units.

-     If properly analyzed and interprets, financial statement can provide valuable insight into a firm's performance.
-     According to my opinion and observation I felt that the future of this textile is very bright.

8. **Title**   :- " A study of profitability analysis Cement companies of India"

Researcher	:-	Urvashi D. Daiya
Year	:-	2009
Degree	:-	Master Of Philosophy in commerce
University	:-	K.S.K.V. Kachchh University
Objective	:-	The main objective at the study.

-     To understand Profitability analysis and it's conceptual framework
-     To evaluate the Profitability analysis with financial statements

Universe	:-	Cement Industry
Sampling	:-	APCL, DCL, DCBL, MCL AND UTCL
Research Method	:-	Financial statement analysis and t-test used.

Conclusion :-

-     We can conclude that the performance of companies is poor who get Rank-1
-     Performance satisfactory who get Rank – 2
-     And get good Performance with Rank – 3
-     Here APCL & DCL shows poor Performance while DCBL & MCL shows satisfactory Performance.
-     UTCL Ranks the best showing good performance.

9. **Title** :- " Analysis of financial Statements – A study of B.M.C.B & B.C.C.B in Bhuj City"

Researcher :- Gandhi Ridhdhi. V

Year :- 2010

Degree :- Master Of Philosophy in commerce

University :- K.S.K.V. Kachchh University

Objective :- The main objective at the study.

- To understand financial analysis and it's conceptual framework
- To evaluate the financial analysis with financial statements
- To B.M.C.B & B.C.C.B at banking industry

Universe :- Banking Industry

Sampling :- B.M.C.B & B.C.C.B at bhuj city

Research Method :- Financial statement analysis and t-test used.

Conclusion :-

- The liquid Asset to Demand Deposit Ratio of BMCB is very lower i.e reduced to less than 1. which is very riskier for deposit holders while BCCB has try to Maintain at 1. So BMCB should try to maintain the same

- Interest earnings and deposits of BCCB are lawer than BMCB. BCCB tried to improve the interest earning to total fund Ratio. BCCB has improved the interest earning to total fund Ratio in the year 2008. But still it is lawer than BMCB Eventhough there is scope for BCCB to improve the ratio.

- Earning per share of BMCB and BCCB banks were reducing drastically year by year during the five years so both the bank should improve the EPS by increasing the total earnings.

10. **Title** :- " A Comparative study of financial analysis

Of Two companies of Mining Industry (with reference To G.M.D.C & N.M.D.C)

Researcher	:-	Thacker kajal. L
Year	:-	2009
Degree	:-	Master Of Philosophy in commerce
University	:-	K.S.K.V. Kachchh University
Objective	:-	The main objective at the study.

- To understand financial analysis and it's conceptual framework
- To evaluate the financial analysis with financial statements
- To G.M.D.C & N.M.D.C at Mining Industry

Universe	:-	Mining Industry
Sampling	:-	G.M.D.C & N.M.D.C
Research Method	:-	Financial statement analysis, F-test and t-test used.

Conclusion   :-

- In this study G.M.D.C is more efficient to N.M.D.C
- The liquidity ratio of G.M.D.C is high to G.M.D.C
- The profitability of G.M.D.C is very good.

11. Comaprative analysis of financial performance of grasim and reliance industries limited by chudasama mayuri B M.phil 2011 K.S.K.V kachchh university

12. The most recent and pioneering work was done in the year 2002 by Dr. P.S Hirani on "Profitability analysis of paper industry". For this study on profit measurement he has used various tools & techniques.

13. Dr. S.C.Jain has made a study at profitability and other aspects of financial management at Indian industries.

3.5 Data collection:

For this study we have selected Life Insurance Corporation Of India. The study was based on secondary data. The data relating to the financial statements analysis at the a published annual reports collected data selected Life insurance Corporation of India for the year 2006 to 2010. the secondary data wherever needed opinions journals, magazines, newspapers, accounting, literature on insurance industries have been used in the study for the purpose at analysis at balance sheet and profit and loss account the figures taken from annual reports.

3.6 Objective of study

The principal and Main objectives of the study was as under;

1.   To make comparative study of Financial analysis of Life insurance Corporation of India (comparison towards Internal Years)

2.   Investors will know the Financial Analysis of Life insurance Corporation of India

3.   To examine Revenue statement Ratios, Balance sheet Ratios and   Composite Ratios of Life Insurance corporation of India

4.   To examine Liquidity Ratios, Leverage Ratios and Activity Or Efficiency Ratios of selected Life insurance Corporation of India

5.   To evaluate the financial analysis with the help of financial statements of Life Insurance corporation of India.

3.7   Hypothesis of the study

The Main hypothesis of the study was as under;

H_0 The Profitability status of L.I.C remain consistent during period of study.

H_1 Profitability status of L.I.C remain inconsistent during period of study.

3.8 Tools and Techniques used:

The techniques at ratio analysis have been adopted for the purpose at financial analysis at selected Life insurance Corporation of India.

For the present study following tools was used for Analysis of Selected Life Insurance companies.

Accounting Techniques

Ratio analysis:

Ratio is was known and most widely used tool at financial analysis ratio can be defined as "the indicated quotient at tow mathematical expressions an operational definition at ratio is the relationship in a simple mathematical from 'ratio are simple a means at highlighting between figures drawn from financial widely used tool through it has certain limits ratio analysis helps to analyses.

Concept at Variable:

The concern is commonly use in accounting and others calculations. The variable used in the present study was gross profit, operating profit, and net profit, and cash profit, turns over etc.

Statistical Techniques:

Used at statistical techniques has become a normal in any type at analysis. Statistical analysis at tools which used for financial analysis. The researcher picks up the chi-square test specific level at significance for accepting as rejection the null hypothesis the testing hypothesis selecting the various financial analysis at the under study. And mean, standard deviation and co efficient of variation is taken for checking consistency of profitability of L.I.C.

3.9 Chapter Plan

The present research study was divided into Five chapters.

Chapter-1   An overview of Life Insurance Industries

Chapter-2   Conceptual framework of financial
statements analysis

Chapter -3   Research methodology

chapter 4   Analysis of data

Chapter -5   Findings, conclusions & suggestions

3.10 LIMITATIONS AT STUDY

1. The study is based on secondary data taken form published annual reports and website.

2. The study in mainly based on ratio Analysis which have their own limitations

3. The Life Insurance Corporation Of India have been covered for present study other private Life insurance companies are not covered for the study.

4. The study is only covered Life Insurance business, Other huge Non life Insurance sector is not covered.

3.11 REFERENCES

For research purpose

1.	C.R.Kothari	"Research Methodology", Wiley Eastern Limited, 1995.
2.	Gupta S.C.,	"Fundamentals of statistics" , Himalaya Publishing House, 1982.
3.	Dr. R.S Patel.,	"Statistical Methods for Educational Research" Jay Publication 102-103 ognaj, Ahmedabad-380060.

Chapter – 4
Analysis of Data

4.1   Introduction

4.2   Meaning of Ratio analysis

4.3   Nature of Ratio Analysis

4.4   Various methods of classification of Ratios

4.5   Benefits of Ratio Analysis

4.6   Limitation of Ratio analysis

4.7   Meaning of Trend Analysis & Meaning of Common Size Analysis

4.8   Benefits of Trend Analysis

4.9   Limitation of Trend analysis

4.10   Analysis of data

4.10.1   Gross profit Ratio

4.10.2   Net profit Ratio

4.10.3   Operating expenses Ratio

4.10.4   Current Ratio

4.10.5   Earning per share

4.10.6   Return on capital Employed

4.10.7   Return on Proprietor's funds

4.10.8   Long term funds to fixed Assets

4.10.9   Working capital Turn Over

4.10.10   Trend Analysis

4.10.11   Common Size statement

4.11 Reference

4.1   Introduction

Financial Statement are analyzed & criticized through using different methods to measure profitability of business units. Business profitability trends are not concluded simply on a single year financial statement. A systematic attempting made to arrange in comparison last five to seven years particularly profit and loss Account & Balance sheet statements.

After preparation of the financial statements, one may be interested in knowing the position of an enterprise from different points of view. This can be done by analyzing the financial statement with the help of different tools of analysis such as ratio analysis, funds flow analysis, cash flow analysis, comparative statement analysis, etc. Here I have done financial analysis by ratios. In this process, a meaningful relationship is established between two or more accounting figures for comparison.

Financial ratios are widely used for modeling purposes both by practitioners and researchers. The firm involves many interested parties, like the owners, management, personnel, customers, suppliers, competitors, regulatory agencies, and academics, each having their views in applying financial statement analysis in their evaluations. Practitioners use financial ratios, for instance, to forecast the future success of companies, while the researchers' main interest has been to develop models exploiting these ratios. Many distinct areas of research involving financial ratios can be discerned. Historically one can observe several major themes in the financial analysis literature. There is overlapping in the observable themes, and they do not necessarily coincide with what theoretically might be the best founded areas.

Financial statements are those statements which provide information about profitability and financial position of a business. It includes two statements, i.e., profit & loss a/c or income statement and balance sheet or position statement. The income statement presents the summary of the income earned and the expenses incurred during a financial year. Position statement presents the financial position of the business at the end of the year. Before understanding the meaning of analysis of financial statements, it is necessary to understand the meaning of _analysis' and _financial statements'.

Analysis means establishing a meaningful relationship between various items of the two financial statements with each other in such a way that a conclusion is drawn. By financial statements, we mean two statements- (1) profit & loss a/c (2) balance sheet. These are prepared at the end of a given period of time. They are indicators of profitability and financial soundness of the business concern.

Here we are studying Financial Analysis of Life Insurance Corporation of India. We have to use for Financial Analysis different technique of Financial statement Analysis First of all we have to used Ratio Analysis. Secondly used Trend Analysis and at last we have use Common Size Statement Analysis. Under this study we can try to evaluate Profitability position of Life Insurance Corporation Of India.

4.2 Meaning Of Ratio Analysis

According to J.Batty "The term accounting ratio is use to describe significant relationships which exist between figures shown in a balance sheet, in a profit and loss account, in a budgetary control system or in any other past the accounting organization".

The accounting ratios indicate a quantitative relationship which is used for analysis and decision making. It provides basis for inter-firm as well as interfere comparison. The ratios will be effective only when they are compared with ratios at base period at with standards or with the industry ratios.

Ratio analysis is a very powerful analytical tool useful for measuring performance at an organist in the ratio analysis concentrates on the inter-relationship among the figures appearing in the aforementioned four financial statements.

Ratio analysis allow interested parties like shareholder's, investors, creditors government and analysts to make an evaluation at certain aspects at a firm's performance ratios are considered to be the best guides for the efficient executing at basis managerial functions like planning forecasting and control etc. ratio analysis is extremely helpful in providing valuable insight into a company's financial picture.

4.3 Nature at Ratio analysis:

Ratios are designed to show how one number is related to another it is worked out by dividing one number by another ratios are customarily presented either in the form at a coefficient or a percentage or as a proportion for example, the current assets and current liabilities of a business in a particular date are rest. 2 lacks and rest. 1 laky at respectively. The resulting ratio at current and current liabilities could be expressed as 2 (i.e. 200000/100000) or as 200 percent alternatively in the form at a proportion the same ratio may be expressed as 2:1 , i.e., the current assets are two times the current liabilities

4.4 Various methods at classification of ratios:

Ratios may be classified in a number at ways to suit any particular purpose. Different kinds at ratios are selected for different types of situation, mostly, the purposes for which the ratios are used and the kind at data available determine the nature at analysis in generally, the following bases at classification are:

(A) Classification According Accounting Statements.

This classification is based on the nature at accounting used for compiling ratios appears accordingly, the different subdivisions are:

1. **Balance sheet Ratios:**

   These ratios are also called as financial ratios. The components as items for computations at these ratios are drawn from the balance sheet examples. Current ratio (items used for computation are current assets and current liabilities debt-equity ratio (items are long term debts and shareholder's funds

2. **Revenue Ratios:**

   These ratios are also called as operating ratios. The items used for the   calculation at these ratios are usually taken cut from the income statement i.e., trading and profit and loss account, examples are gross profit ratio, net profit ratio, operating ratio, etc.

3. **Inter-statement Ratios or combined Ratios:**

   The information required for the computation at these ratios is normally drawn from both balance sheet and trading and profit and loss account examples are debtors turnover ratio, Fixed Assets Turn Over, Working Capital Turn over.

   (B) Classification According to time:

   This classification is based on the point at time in relation to which ratios are compiled accordingly; they may be classified as follows:

1. **Structural Ratios:**

   The data used for the computations at these ratios normally relate to the save point e.g., ratios at a particular month, quarter as year. In this sense, the balance sheet ratios, and the income statement ratios at a particular year may be termed as structural ratios

2.   **Trend Ratios:**

These ratios are computed between items over a period at time and used for the analysis. For example, current ratio for a period at 10 years may be calculated and the trend (long –term changes) observed from, this ratio may be used for the analysis

(C) Classification According to Importance:

Some ratios when related to the main objective of the business for the purpose at analysis may be yore important than others the British institute at management has recommended this basis. At classification for inters-firm comparison and the institute has suggested the following types

1. Primary Ratio:

The prime motive an any business undertaking is profit and therefore, ratios like profit to sales return on capital employed may be termed as primary ratios for such undertakings.

2. Secondary Ratios:

These ratios are mainly used to explain the primary ratios. They are also known as subsidiary or succoring ratios. Taking the ratio at return on capital employed as the primary ratios, the following ratios may be grouped as secondary trios. (a) Profit and earning ratios (b) cost or expenses ratios; (c) capital and seated ratios and turnover ratios.

(D) Classification According to Function Or Tests Satisfied:

Robert. N. Antonym suggested that ratios may be grouped on the basis at certain tests, which satisfy the needs at the [arties laving financial interest in the business concern. These tests are (I) test at liquidity (ii) Test at profitability and (iii) market tests.

(E) Classification According to Nature:

Under this classification ratios are grouped as follows,

1. Liquidity Ratios:

The liquidity ratios measure the liquidity at the firm and its ability to meet its maturing short-tem obligations the important ratios in measuring short-tem solvency are (1) current ratio (2) quick ratio (3) Absolute liquidity ratio, and (4) Defensive- Interval Ratio

2. Leverage Ratios:

The long-tem financial stability at the firm may be considered as dependent upon its ability to meet all its inabilities including those not currently payable the ratios which are important measuring the financial leverage of the company is as follows, debt equity ratio, shareholders equity ratio long term debt to shareholders net worth ratio, fixed assets to Fixed Assets ratio.

3. Turn Over Or Activity Ratios:

These ratios enable measurement at the effectiveness at the usage at resources at the command at the concern. Examples fixed assets turnover ratio, stock turnover ratio. These ratios would also indicate the profitability position at the business.

4. Profitability Ratios:

The purpose at study and analysis at profitability ratios are to help assessing the adequacy at profits ensured by the company and also to discover whether profitability is increasing as declining these ratios are intense to measure the end result at business operations examples, gross profit ratio, return on capital employed and operating ratio.

4.5   Benefits of Ratio Analysis

Ratio analysis is an important and age-old technique of financial analysis. The following are some of the advantages of ratio analysis:

1. Simplifies financial statements:

It simplifies the comprehension of financial statements. Ratios tell the whole story of changes in the financial condition of the business.

2. Facilitates inter-firm comparison:

It provides data for inter-firm comparison. Ratios highlight the factors associated with successful and unsuccessful firm. They also reveal strong firms and weak firms, overvalued and undervalued firms.

3. Helps in planning:

It helps in planning and forecasting. Ratios can assist management, in its basic functions of forecasting. Planning, co-ordination, control and communications.

4. Makes inter-firm comparison possible:

Ratios analysis also makes possible comparison of the performance of different divisions of the firm. The ratios are helpful in deciding about their efficiency or otherwise in the past and likely performance in the future.

5. Help in investment decisions:

It helps in investment decisions in the case of investors and lending decisions in the case of bankers etc.

4.6   Limitation of Ratio Analysis

The ratios analysis is one of the most powerful tools of financial management. Though ratios are simple to calculate and easy to understand, they suffer from serious limitations.

1. Limitations of financial statements:

Ratios are based only on the information which has been recorded in the financial statements. Financial statements themselves are subject to several limitations. Thus ratios derived, there from, are also subject to those limitations. For example, non-financial changes though important for the business are not relevant by the financial statements. Financial statements are affected to a very great extent by accounting conventions and concepts. Personal judgment plays a great part in determining the figures for financial statements.

2. Comparative study required:

Ratios are useful in judging the efficiency of the business only when they are compared with past results of the business.

However, such a comparison only provide glimpse of the past performance and forecasts for future may not prove correct since several other factors like market conditions, management policies, etc. may affect the future operations.

3. **Problems of price level changes:**

A change in price level can affect the validity of ratios calculated for different time periods. In such a case the ratio analysis may not clearly indicate the trend in solvency and profitability of the company. The financial statements, therefore, be adjusted keeping in view the price level changes if a meaningful comparison is to be made through accounting ratios.

4. **Lack of adequate standard:**

No fixed standard can be laid down for ideal ratios. There are no well accepted standards or rule of thumb for all ratios which can be accepted as norm. It renders interpretation of the ratios difficult.

5. **Limited use of single ratios:**

A single ratio, usually, does not convey much of a sense. To make a better interpretation, a number of ratios have to be calculated which is likely to confuse the analyst than help him in making any good decision.

6. **Personal bias:**

Ratios are only means of financial analysis and not an end in itself. Ratios have to interpret and different people may interpret the same ratio in different way.

7. **Incomparable:**

Not only industries differ in their nature, but also the firms of the similar business widely differ in their size and accounting procedures etc. It makes comparison of ratios difficult and misleading.

4.7   Meaning of Trend Analysis & Meaning of Common Size Analysis

- **Meaning of Trend Analysis**

    Trend Percentage is also an important tool for analyzing and examining financial statements. Trend Percentage are used to evaluate differences in accounting facts. Generally From amongst the years of which information is gathered, beginning year is assumed as base year and with that assumption, data for the remaining years are examined, trend percentage is walked out in comparison with base year. It is important to note that in such cases base year calculated must be normal year i.e. irrespective of any happenings like war, cyclone, recession, business disaster etc.

- **Meaning of Common Size Analysis**

    A company financial statement that displays all items as percentages of a common base figure. This type of financial statement allows for easy analysis between companies or between time periods of a company. The values on the common size statement are expressed as percentages of a statement component such as revenue. While most firms don't report their statements in common size, it is beneficial to compute if you want to analyze two or more companies of differing size against each other.

    Formatting financial statements in this way reduces the bias that can occur when analyzing companies of differing sizes. It also allows for the analysis of a company over various time periods, revealing, for example, what percentage of sales is cost of goods sold and how that value has changed over time.

4.8 Benefits of Trend Analysis

1. This trend percentage is advantageous as analyzing tool as it provides the advantages of summarization and substitution of large volumes.

2.   This percentage enables the researcher to have appropriate guidance in respect of differences observed in personal property, liability and Net Assets over a period of time.

3.   It is easy to interpreted of data and also to have gist of comparative analysis.

4.   Trend indicated directions of movements of a company. The data is useful to have meaningful interpretation and also helps to conclude have scientific conclusion regarding economic viability of a company.

5.   The added advantage of trend projection is to have clarity of management. It adds to the understanding of company's Philosophy, policy & motivating factors

6.   Trend analysis is useful to have clarity of logical relationship found in financial statements. It expresses advantageous for the company. It trends reflects an improvement in inventory cost along with positive change in sales numbers and in reverse it is proved disadvantageous.

4.9   Limitation of Trend Analysis

1.   It is the biggest limitation of the method that is fails to expose clearly whether the changes occurred over a period of time are in the interest of the company or not.

2.   Trend numbers are presented as index numbers having percentage changes. This percentage method has its own statistical limitations.

3.   The method does not become meaningful unless accounting principles and methods are not followed constantly during period of study.

4.   It is likely to mislead it the data is not strongly supported by absolute numbers.

5.   This method ignores in principle price changes observed during the time of study period.

4.10 Analysis Of Data

The purpose at study and analysis at profitability ratios are help assessing the adequacy at profits earned by the company and also to discover whether profitability is increasing or declining the profitable at the firm is the net result at a large number at policies and decisions. The profitability ratios show the combined effects at liquidity, asset management and debt management on operating results. Profitability ratios measured with senescence to sales, capital employed, total assets employed, shareholders. Hands etc. The major profitability ratios are:

4.10.1   Gross profit Ratio

G.P ratio is the ratio of gross profit to net sales express as a percentage it expresses the relationship between gross profit margin and sales. The basic components are gross profit & net sales means Total sales less sales return. Gross profit would be the difference between Net sales and cost of goods sold.

In trading concern, the cost of goods sold would be equal to opening stock plus purchases and all direct expenses relating to purchases minus closing stock..

In case of manufacturing concerns it would be equal to stock plus cost of production minus closing stock.

In life insurance company it is a service providing sector concerns would be gross profit is equal to surplus and net sales is equal to Net premium which premium less re insurance ceded and add reinsurance accepted.

$$\text{Gross profit ratio} = \frac{\text{Gross profit(surplus)}}{\text{Net Sales (Net premium)}} * 100$$

Analysis at Gross profit pared at selected companies
Table No. 4.1

Gross profit Life Insurance Corporation of India for the Period from 2006 to 2010

Years	Surplus	Net Premium	Gross Profit
2006	6217705	907591972	0.69
2007	7578089	1277822594	0.59
2008	8295897	149705581	0.55
2009	9291158	1571865504	0.59
2010	10309227	1859859122	0.55
N = 5			$\sum Xi$ = 2.97

Source: Computed from the annual report and accounts at selected companies.

$$\overline{X} = \frac{\sum Xi}{N} = \frac{2.97}{5} = 0.595$$

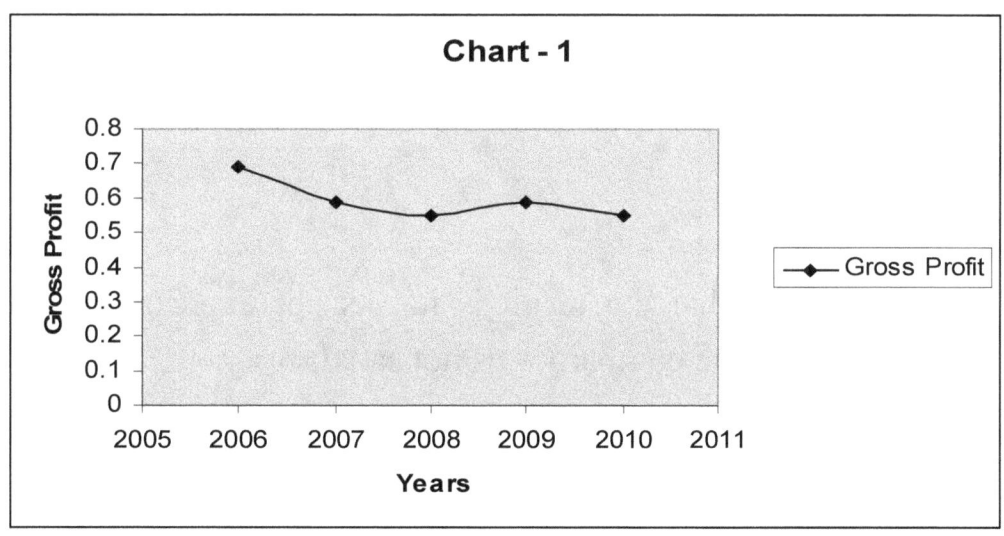

As indicated in table No - 4.1 and Chart – 1 the percentage of gross profit ratio was found decreased trend as compared to 2006.

In 2006 the gross profit ratio was 0.69% which decreased by 0.10% to 59%. Another 0.04% decreased in 2008 to 55%. While minor increment by 0.04% to 0.50% in 2009. In last which again decreased by 0.04% to 0.55% in 2010.

The average Gross profit Ratio of Life Insurance Corporation Of India is 0.59%

The highest gross profit ratio at Life Insurance Corporation Of India is 0.69% in the year at 2006. The lowest gross profit ratio of Life Insurance Corporation Of India is 0.55% in the year of 2008 & 2010 at 2006 and 2010.

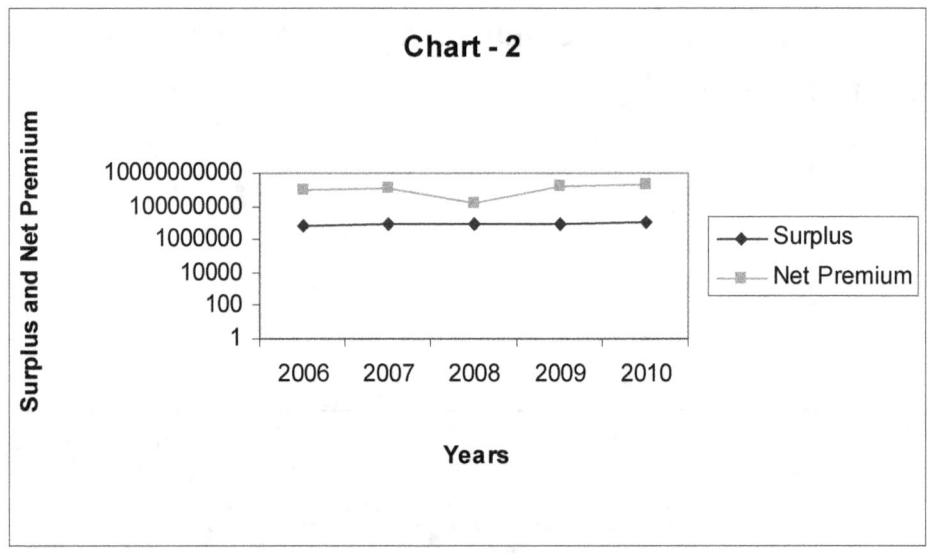

So we can say that the result is not as per expectations. And the performance of the company was not satisfactory.

4.10.2   Net profit Ratio

N.P ratio is the ratio of Net income or Net profit After taxes To Net sales. Net profit as used here is the balance of profit and loss account (shareholder's account) which is arrived after considering all Income from investments (shareholder's funds income), other income and indirect expenses etc.,

$$\text{Net profit ratio} = \frac{\text{Net profit}}{\text{Net premium}} * 100$$

This is used as measure at overall profitability and is useful to the owners.

Analysis at Net profit pared at selected companies

Table No. 4.2

Net profit Life Insurance Corporation of India for the Period from 2006 to 2010

Years	Net Profit after taxes	Net Premium	Net Profit
2006	6315801	907591972	0.70
2007	7736203	1277822594	0.61
2008	8446259	149705581	0.5641
2009	9573488	1571865504	0.609
2010	10607168	1859859122	0.57
N = 5			∑Xi=3.0531

Source: Computed from the annual report and accounts at selected companies.

$$\overline{X} = \frac{\sum Xi}{N} = \frac{3.0531}{5} = 0.61062$$

Chart – 3

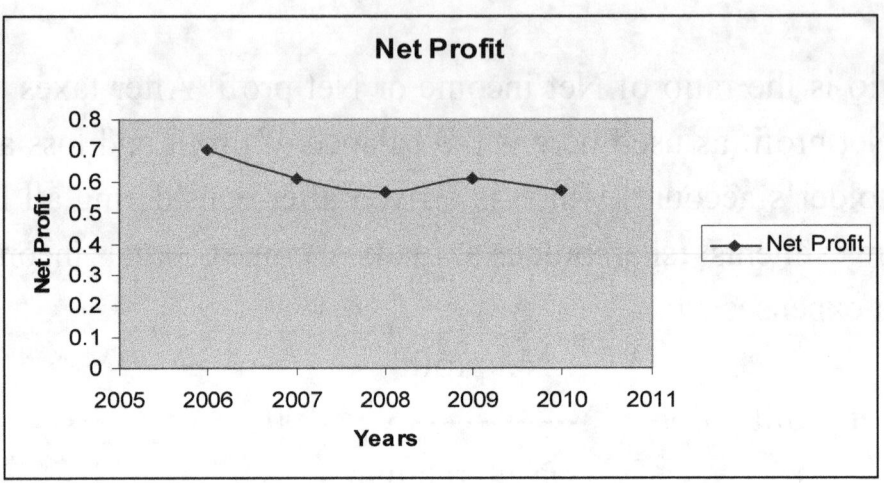

As indicated in table 4.2 and Chart – 2 the percentage of Net profit ratio was found decreased trend as compared to 2006.

In 2006 the Net profit ratio was 0.70% which is decreased by 0.09% to 0.61% in year 2007. Again decreased by 0.09% to 0.5641% in 2008. which is increased by 0.0449% to 0.609% in 2009. And at last again decreased by 0.039% to 0.57% in year 2010.

The average Net profit Ratio of Life Insurance Corporation Of India is 0.61062%.

The highest Net profit ratio at Life Insurance Corporation Of India is 0.70% in the year at 2006. The lowest Net profit ratio of Life Insurance Corporation Of India is 0.5641% in the year of 2008 at 2006 and 2010.

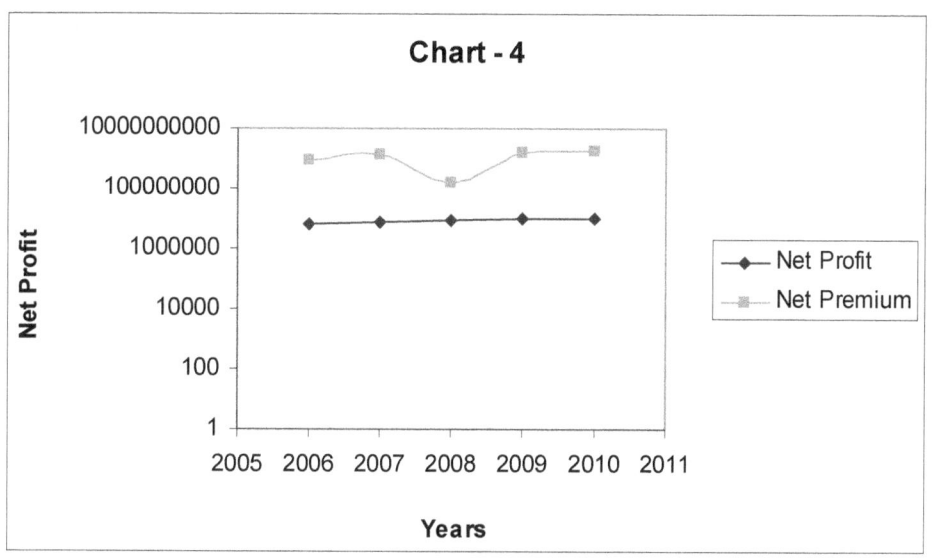

4.10.3   Operating expenses Ratio

This is the ratio of operating cost to Net sales. The term operating cost retests to cost of goods sold plus operating expenses.

The main are operating cost and Net sales operating expenses normally include the following item's

(a)   office and administration expenses

(b)   selling and distribution expenses

financial changes such as interest, provision for doubtful debts, other expenses., generally excluded from operating expenses.

$$\text{Operating Ratio} = \frac{\text{Operating cost}}{\text{Net premium}} * 100$$

$$\text{Operating Ratio} = \frac{\text{Commission} + \text{Operating expenses}}{\text{Net premium}} * 100$$

This is used as measure at overall profitability and it is useful to the owner's.

Analysis at operating Expenses Ratio at selected companies
Table No. 4.3

Operating expenses ratio of Life Insurance Corporation of India for the Period from 2006 to 2010

Years	Commission + Operating expenses	Net Premium	Operating Expenses Ratio
2006	131364800	907591972	14.17
2007	162549079	1277822594	12.72
2008	178774172	149705581	11.94
2009	190975307	1571865504	12.15
2010	243561370	1859859122	13.096
N = 5			$\sum Xi = 64.076$

Source: Computed from the annual report and accounts at selected companies.

$$\overline{X} = \frac{\sum Xi}{N} = \frac{64.076}{5} = 12.82$$

Chart – 5

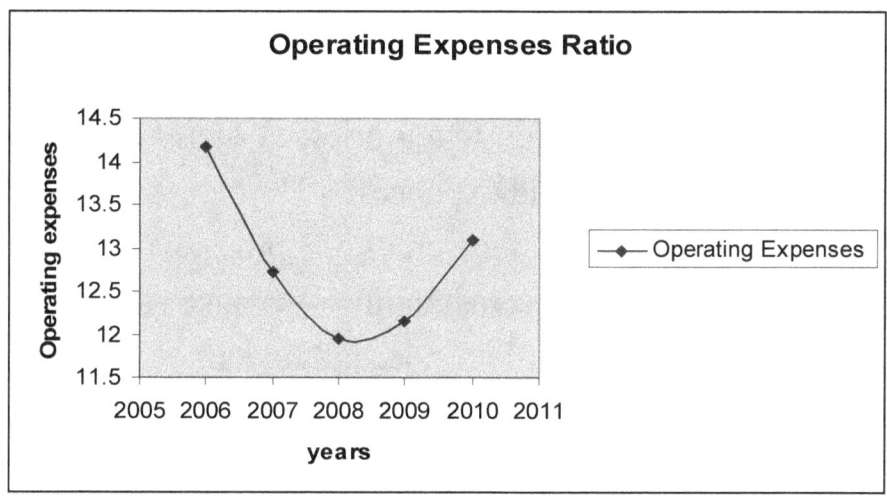

As indicated in table 4.3 and Chart – 3 the percentage of operating expenses ratio was found decreased to increased trend as compared to 2006.

In 2006, the operating expenses ratio was 14.47% . This was decreased to 12.72% in 2007. Again it was decreased by 0.78% to 11.94% in 2008. While minor increment by 0.21% in 200 in 2009. And at last again increased by 0.946& to 13.096% in year 2010.

The average operating expenses ratio of Life Insurance Corporation Of India is 12.82%

The highest operating expenses ratio at Life Insurance Corporation Of India is 14.17% in the year at 2006. The lowest operating expenses ratio of Life Insurance Corporation Of India is 11.94% in the year of 2008 at 2006 and 2010.

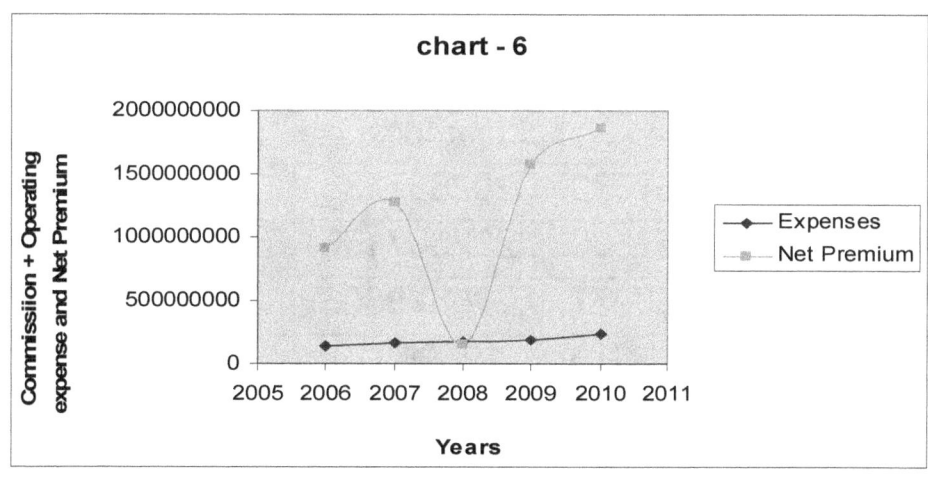

4.10.4   Current Ratio

The current assets include cash and Bank Balance, Marketable securities, Bills, Receivable, Inventories, Loans and advances, Advances Payment and prepaid expenses.

The current liabilities include creditors, bills payable bank overdraft short-term loans, outstanding expense & income tax payable, unclaimed divided and proposed dividend.

The current ratio measures the ability of the firm to meet its current liabilities. The current assets get converted into cash into the operational cycle of the firm and provide the fund needed to pay current liabilities. The higher the ratio, to ward off.

Current Ratio is the ratio of current Assets to current liabilities express as a percentage it expresses the relationship between current assets and current liabilities.

$$\text{Current Ratio} = \frac{\text{Current Assets}}{\text{Current liabilities}}$$

This is used as measure at overall profitability and it is useful to the owner's.

Analysis at Current Ratio at selected companies

Table No. 4.4

Current Ratio of Life Insurance Corporation of India for the Period from 2006 to 2010

Years	Current Assets	Current Liabilities	Current Ratio
2006	343157380	202667136	1.69
2007	343157380	202667136	1.69
2008	427950277	220878503	1.94
2009	487146675	19590219	2.49
2010	494780941	219021982	2.26
N = 5			$\sum Xi = 10.07$

<u>**Source:**</u> Computed from the annual report and accounts at selected companies.

$$\overline{X} = \frac{\sum Xi}{N} = \frac{10.07}{5} = 2.0104$$

Chart –7

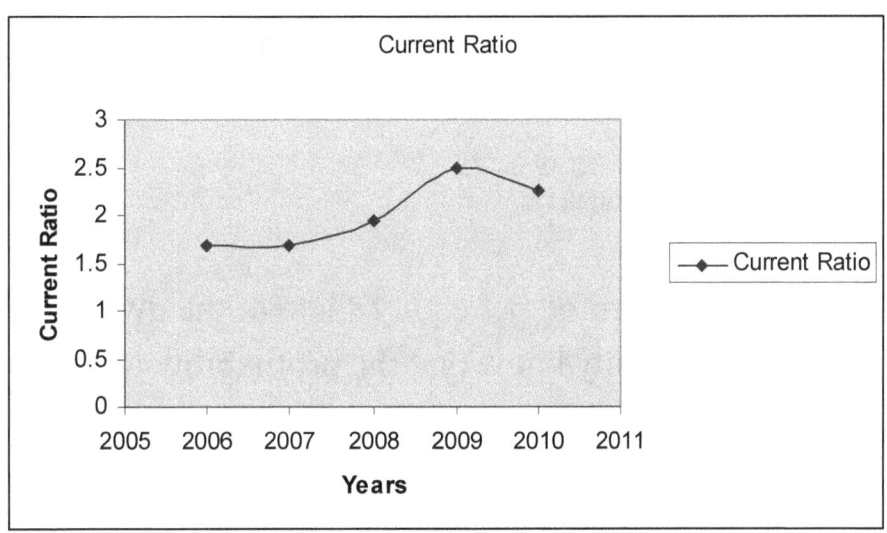

As indicated in table 4.3 and Chart – 4 the Current ratio was found increased trend as compared to 2006.

This was found 1.69 in 2006. which was same on 2007. This was increased by 0.25 to 1.94 in 2008. Again increased by 0.55 to 2.49 in 2009. At last decreasion by 0.23 in increasion to 2.26 in 2010.

The average Current ratio of Life Insurance Corporation Of India is 2.0104

The highest Current ratio at Life Insurance Corporation Of India is 2.49 in the year at 2009. The lowest operating expenses ratio of Life Insurance Corporation Of India is 1.69 in the year of 2006 and 2007 at 2006 and 2010.

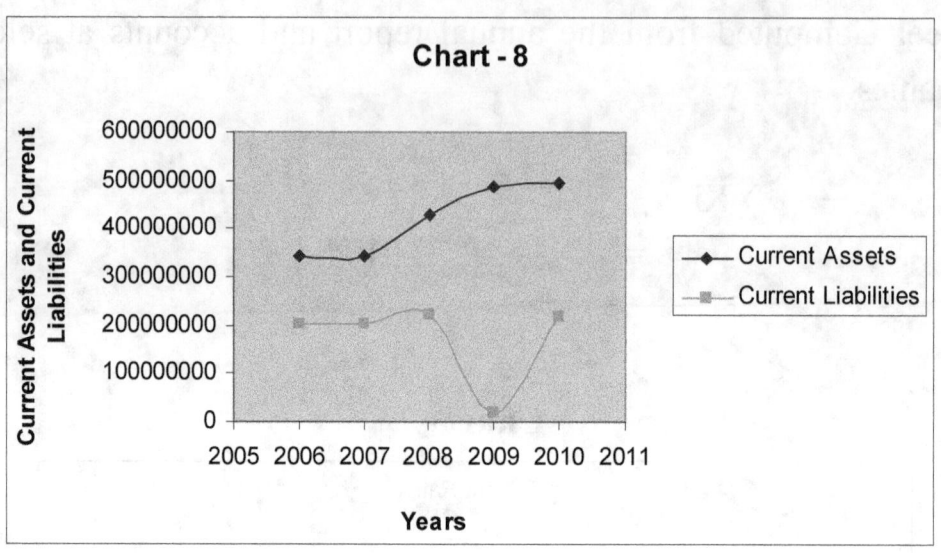

4.10.5 Earning per share

E.P.S is ratio of earning per equity share of the owners. With the help of E.P.S we can easily know that the profitability of the company and valuation of shareholders.

$$\text{E.P.S} = \frac{\text{Net profit (After interest and taxes)}}{\text{Number of Equity shares}}$$

This is used as measure at overall profitability and it is useful to the owner's.

Analysis at E.P.S at selected companies

Table No. 4.5

E.P.S of Life Insurance Corporation of India for the Period from 2006 to 2010

Years	Net Profit after taxes	Number of Shares	EPS
2006	6315801	5000000	1263.16

2007	7736203	5000000	1547.24
2008	8446259	5000000	1689.25
2009	9573488	5000000	1914.70
2010	10607168	5000000	2121.43
N = 5			$\sum Xi=8535.78$

Source: Computed from the annual report and accounts at selected companies.

$$\overline{X} = \frac{\sum Xi}{N} = \frac{8535.78}{5} = 1707.156$$

Chart – 9

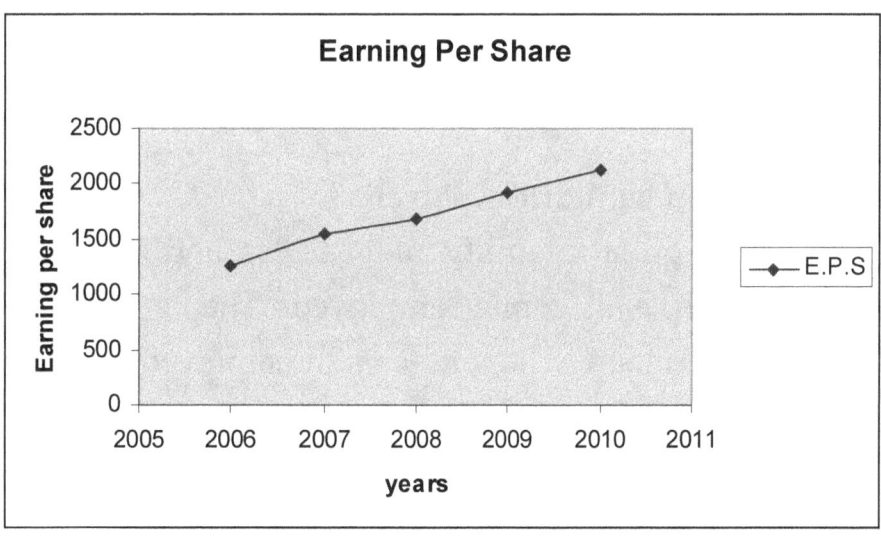

As indicated in table 4.5 and Chart – 5 the Earning per share was found increased trend as compared to 2006.

In year 2006 E.P.S was 1263.16. which increased to 1547.24 in 2007. This further increased to 1689.25 in 2008. which again increased to 1914.70 in 2009. At last it was increased to 2121.23 in 2010.

The average E.P.S of Life Insurance Corporation Of India is 1707.156.

The highest E.P.S at Life Insurance Corporation Of India is 2121.43 in the year at 2010. The lowest E.P.S of Life Insurance Corporation Of India is 1263.16 in the year of 2006 at 2006 and 2010.

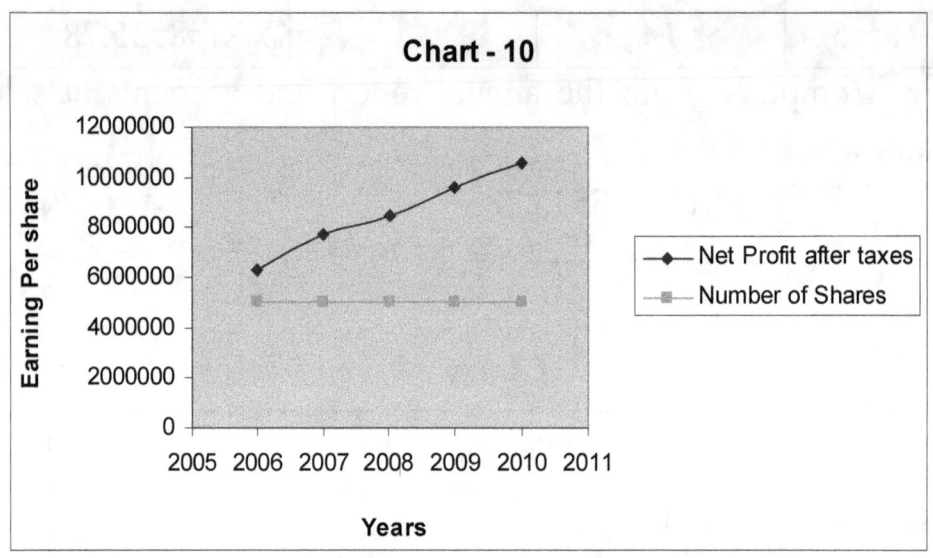

Chart - 10

4.10.6   Return on capital Employed

It is an index of profitability of business and is obtained by comparing net profit with capital employed. The ratio is normally expressed in the percentage. The term capital employed includes share capital , reserve and long term liabilities

$$\text{Net profit ratio} = \frac{\text{Net profit(before taxes)}}{\text{Share capital} + \text{Reserve} + \text{Borrowings}}$$

The success or otherwise of the enterprise is judged with the help of this ratio. It is perhaps the most important ratio from the view point of management.

Analysis at Return on capital Employed pared at selected companies

Table No. 4.6

Return on capital Employed Life Insurance Corporation of India for the Period from 2006 to 2010

Years	Net Profit before taxes	Share capital + Reserve + Borrowings	Return on Capital Employed
2006	6315801	1769985	25.99
2007	7736203	2928099	18.58
2008	8446259	3078461	14.15
2009	9573488	3360791	12.81
2010	10607168	3658732	12.81
N = 5			$\sum Xi = 84.34$

Source: Computed from the annual report and accounts at selected companies.

$$\overline{X} = \frac{\sum Xi}{N} = \frac{84.34}{5} = 16.87$$

Chart – 11

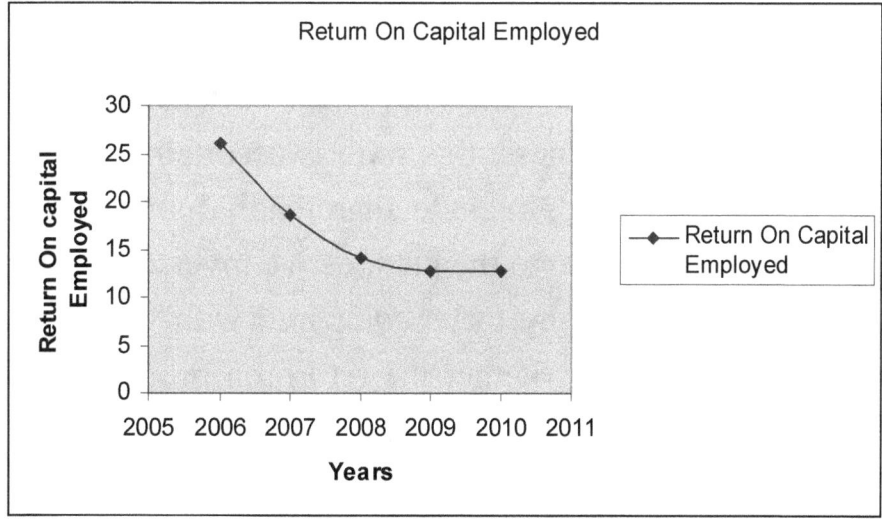

As indicated in table 4.6 and Chart – 6 Return on capital employed was found decreased trend as compared to 2006.

In 2006 , it was 25.99, This was decreased by 7.41 to 18.58 in 2007. which was 14.15 in 2008. This further decreased by 1.34 to 12.81in 2009. At last it was 12.81 in 2010.

The average Return on capital Employed of Life Insurance Corporation Of India is 16.87.

The highest Return on capital Employed at Life Insurance Corporation Of India is 25.99in the year at 2010. The lowest Return on capital Employed of Life Insurance Corporation Of India is 12.81 in the year of 2009 and 2010

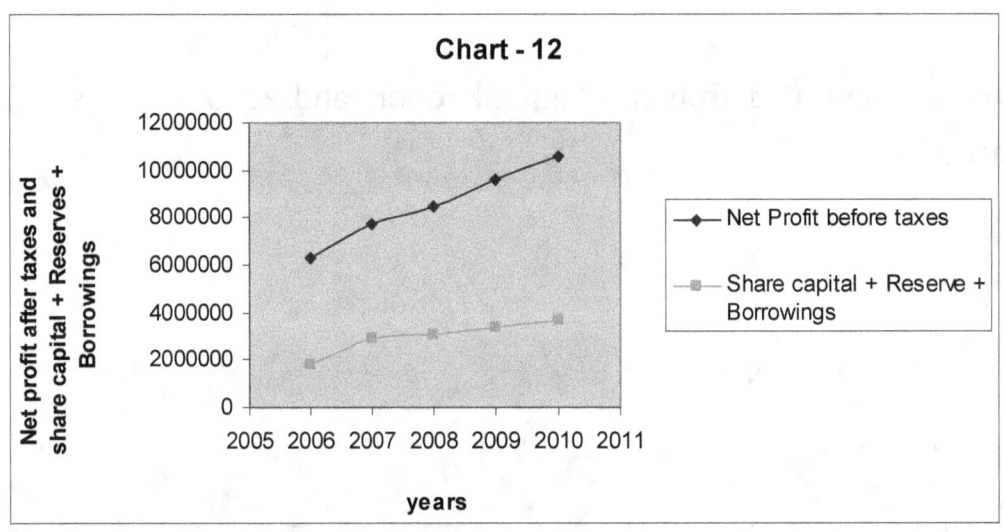

4.10.7   Return on Proprietor's funds

In order to judge the efficiency with which the proprietors' funds are employed in business, this ratio is ascertained. Proprietor's Equity or Proprietors' Funds include share capital and reserves. It is of great practical importance to the prospective investors, as it enables the profitability of a company to be compared with that of the other company. It also indicates whether the return on proprietors funds is enough in relation to the risks that they undertake. This ratio shows what amount of dividend is likely to be received on shares. Naturally when return on shareholder's funds is to be calculated. The profit should be after interest and tax i.e., PAT – profit after tax. This ratio usually expressed in percentage.

$$\text{Return on Proprietor's funds} = \frac{\text{Net profit After Taxes}}{\text{Share capital} + \text{Reserves}} * 100$$

This is used as measure at overall profitability and is useful to the owners.

Analysis at Return on Proprietor's funds pared at selected companies

Table No. 4.7

Return on Proprietor's funds Life Insurance Corporation of India for the Period from 2006 to 2010

Years	Net Profit After taxes	Share capital + Reserve	Return On Proprietor's funds
2006	6315801	1769985	3.57
2007	7736203	2928099	2.642
2008	8446259	3078461	2.7437
2009	9573488	3360791	2.85
2010	10607168	3658732	2.89
N = 5	42678919		$\sum Xi$=14.6957

Source: Computed from the annual report and accounts at selected companies.

$$\overline{X} = \frac{\sum Xi}{N} = \frac{14.6957}{5} = 2.94$$

Chart – 13

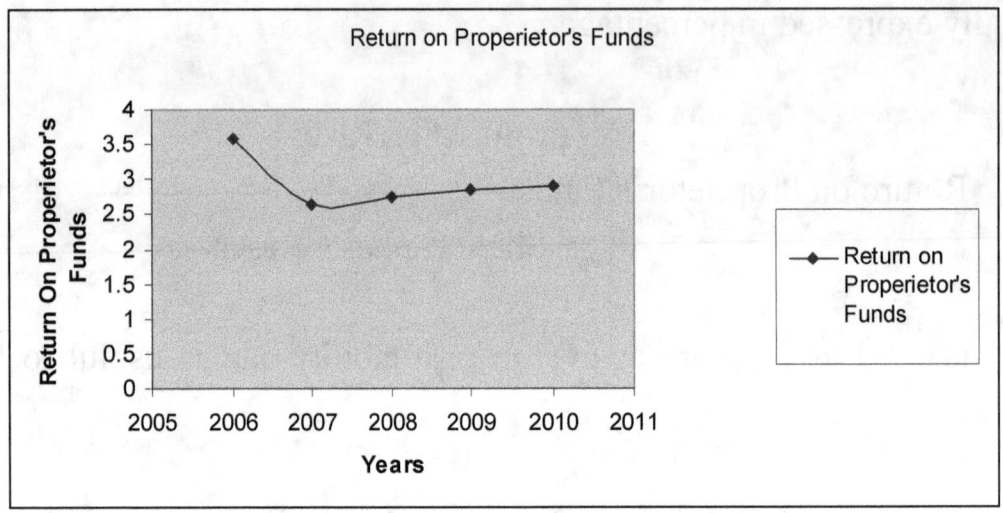

As indicated in table 4.7 and Chart – 7 Return on proprietor's funds was found decreased trend as compared to 2006.

In 2006 , it was 3.57%, This was decreased by 0.928% to 2.642% in 2007. which was 2.7437% in 2008. This further increased by 0.11% to 2.85%in 2009. At last it was 2.89% in 2010.

The average Return on capital Employed of Life Insurance Corporation Of India is 2.94%.

The highest Return on proprietor's funds at Life Insurance Corporation Of India is 2.89 in the year at 2010. The lowest Return on proprietor's funds of Life Insurance Corporation Of India is 2.642 in the year of 2007 at 2006 and 2010.

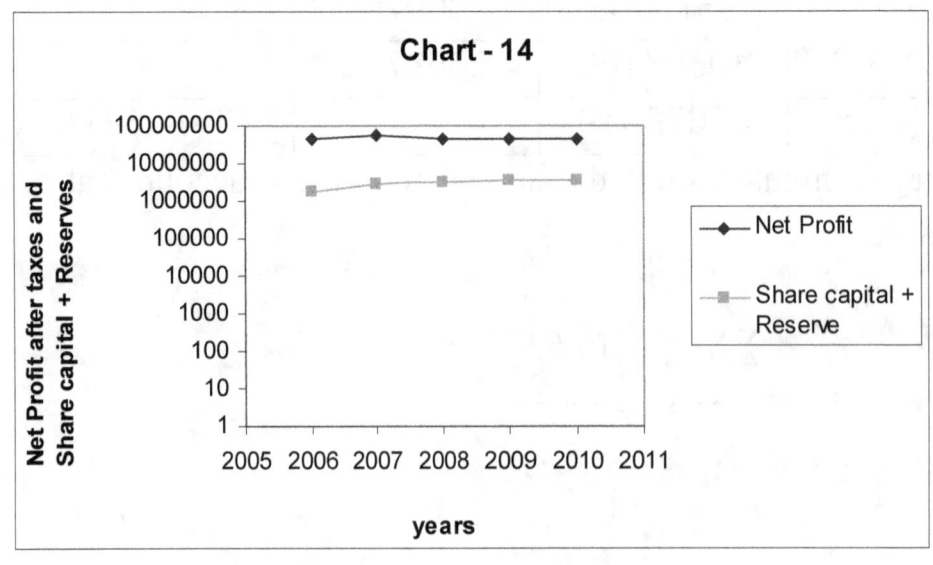

4.10.8   Long term funds to fixed Assets

Normally, the fixed assets of business must be purchased out of fixed capital only, which includes share capital, reserves and long term liabilities. This ratio therefore shows the relationship between fixed capital and fixed assets.

Long term funds to
fixed Assets

$$= \frac{\text{Proprietor's funds} + \text{Borrowings}}{\text{Fixed Assets}} * 100$$

This is used as measure at overall profitability and is useful to the owners.

Analysis at Long term funds to fixed Assets pared at selected companies

Table No. 4.8

Long term funds to fixed Assets Life Insurance Corporation of India for the Period from 2006 to 2010

Years	Proprietor's funds + Borrowings	Fixed Assets	Long term funds to Fixed Assets
2006	1769985	12621446	14
2007	2928099	14035573	20.86
2008	3078461	21176952	14.54
2009	3360791	29798044	11.28
2010	3658732	31229886	11.72
N = 5			$\sum Xi$=72.4

Source: Computed from the annual report and accounts at selected companies.

$$\overline{X} = \frac{\sum Xi}{N} = \frac{72.4}{5} = 14.48$$

Chart – 15

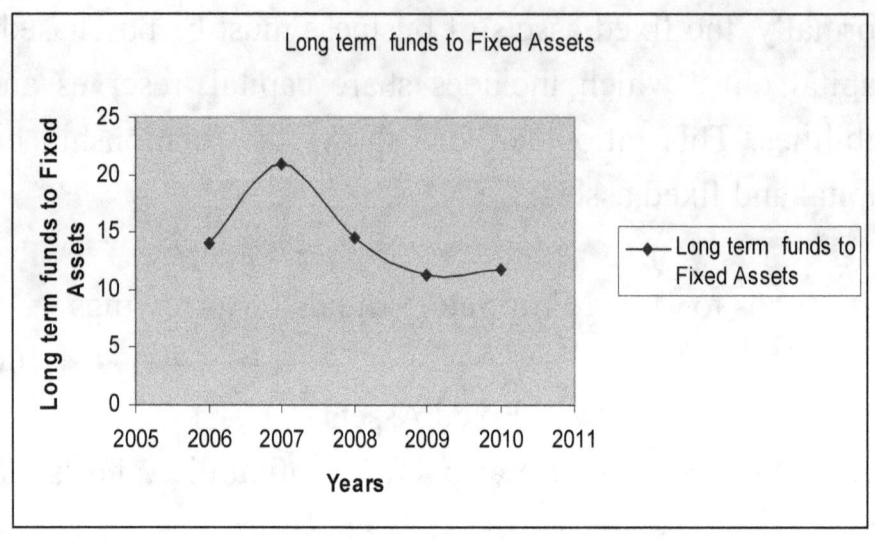

As indicated in table 4.8 and Chart – 8 the percentage of Long term funds to fixed Assets was found increased to decreased trend as compared to 2006.

In 2006 , it was 14%, which is increased to 20.86% in 2007. But it was decreased by 6.32% to 14.54% in 2008. Again decreased by 3.26% to 11.28% in 2009. At last it was 11.72% in 2010.

The average Long term funds to fixed Assets of Life Insurance Corporation Of India is 14.48%.

The highest Long term funds to fixed Assets at Life Insurance Corporation Of India is 20.86% in the year at 2007. The lowest Return on Long term funds to fixed Assets of Life Insurance Corporation Of India is 11.28% in the year of 2009 at 2006 and 2010.

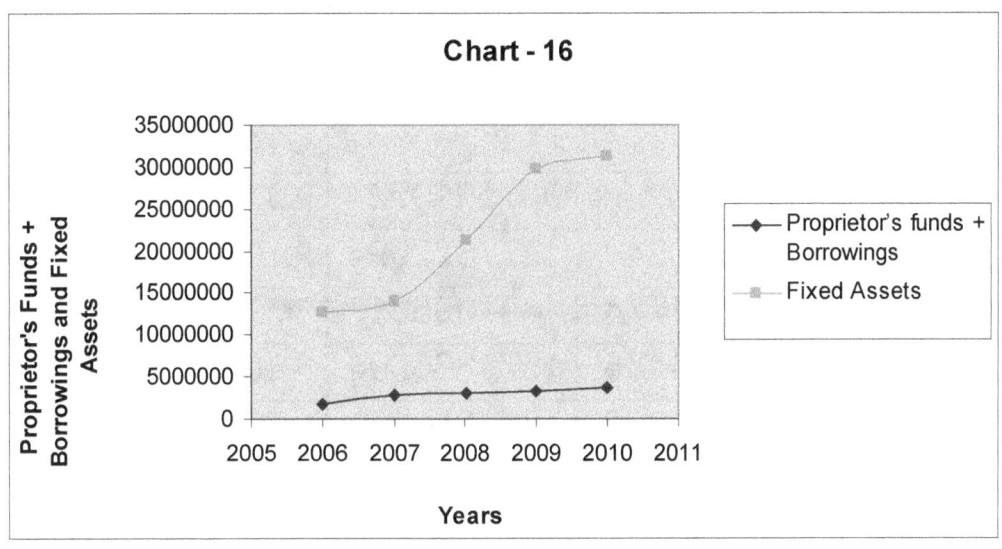

4.10.9 Working capital Turn Over

Working capital means current Assets over current liabilities. (Net working capital is useful for day to day works of a business. Any business the working capital is playing a significant role.

Working capital turn over shows the how much times working capital used by the business. If this turn over is high the profitability of the business is high.

$$\text{Working Capital Turn over} = \frac{\text{Net premium}}{\text{Working capital}} * 100$$

This is used as measure at overall profitability and is useful to the owners.

Analysis at Working Capital Turn over pared at selected companies

Table No. 4.9

Working Capital Turn over of Life Insurance Corporation of India for the Period from 2006 to 2010

Years	Working Capital	Net Premium	Working Capital Turn Over
2006	97357215	907591972	9.32
2007	140490244	1277822594	9.10
2008	207071774	149705581	7.23
2009	291244485	1571865504	5.40
2010	275758959	1859859122	6.75
N = 5			$\sum Xi = 37.8$

Source: Computed from the annual report and accounts at selected companies.

$$\overline{X} = \frac{\sum Xi}{N} = \frac{37.8}{5} = 7.56$$

Chart – 17

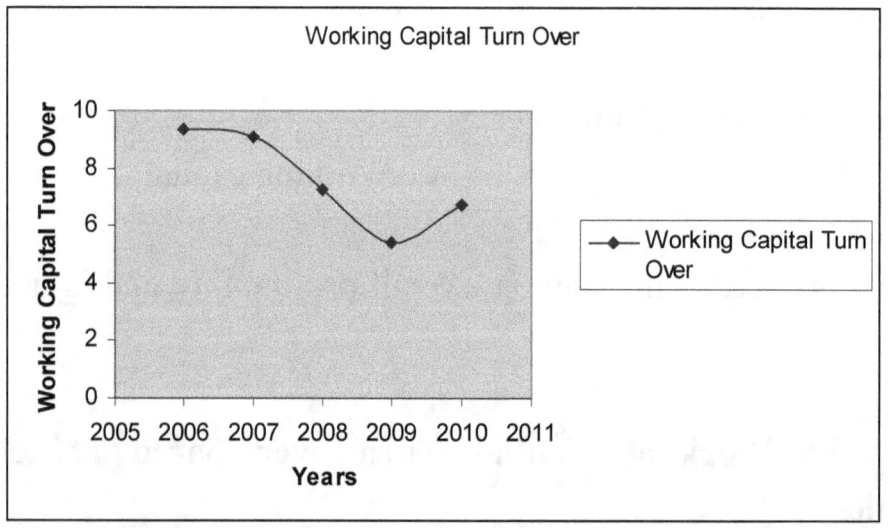

As indicated in table 4.9 and Chart – 9 Working Capital Turn over was found decreased trend as compare to 2006.

This was found 9.32 in 2006. It was decreased to 9.0955 in 2007. Again decreased by 1.8665 to 7.23 in 2008. which again decreased to 5.40 in 2009. And at last it was found increased by 1.353 to 6.75 in 2010

The average Working Capital Turn over of Life Insurance Corporation Of India is 7.56 in 2010.

The highest Working Capital Turn over at Life Insurance Corporation Of India is 9.32 in the year 2006. The lowest Working Capital Turn over of Life Insurance Corporation Of India is 5.40 in the year of 2009.

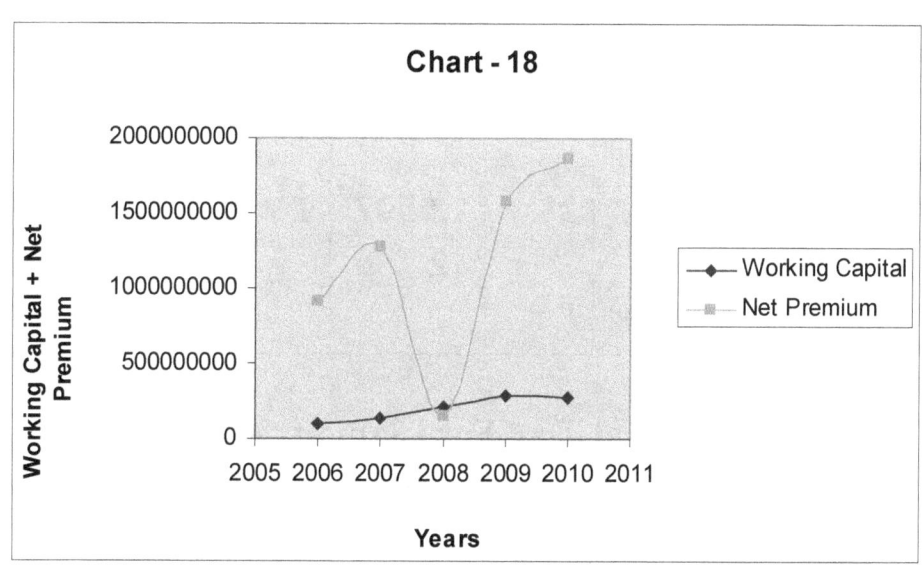

Statistical Tool For Profitability Ratio
Table No :- 4.10

Sr N0.	Particulars	Mean	Rank	Standard Deviation	Rank	Coefficient of Variation	Rank
1	Gross profit	0.594	6	0.057271	5	9.64163	3
2	Net Profit	0.61062	5	0.054327	6	8.897097	2
3	Operating expenses	12.8152	3	0.884853	3	6.904716	1
4	Earning Per share	1707.156	1	330.8034	1	19.37746	5

5	Return On capital Employed	16.868	2	5.622812	2	33.3342	6
6	Return on Proprietor's Funds	2.93914	4	0.365662	4	12.44111	4

Statistical Tool For Efficiency Ratio

1	Long term funds to fixed Assets	14.48	1	3.833927	1	26.4774	2
2	Working capital Turn over	7.56	2	1.650742	2	21.83522	1

Statistical Tool For Liquidity Ratio

Sr N0.	Particulars	Mean	Standard Deviation	Coefficient of Variation
1	Current Ratio	2.014	0.354443	17.59897

Here Rank- 1 indicate the good condition of Rank-2, Rank- 2 indicate the good condition of Rank-3., Rank- 3 indicate the good condition of Rank-4., Rank- 5 indicate the good condition of Rank-6.,

We see in table No- 4.10, Mean of Earning Per share is 1707.156 so it gives a Rank-1, Mean of Return on Capital Employed is 16.868 so it take rank -2, Mean of Operating Expenses is 12.8152 so it take Rank-3, Mean of Return on Proprietor's Funds is 2.93014 so it take Rank – 4, Mean of Net Profit Ratio is 0.61062 so it take Rank-5 and at last Mean of Gross Profit is 0.594 so it take Rank – 6.

Above ranking we conclude that Earning per share is higher than Return on capital Employed, Operating expenses, Return on Proprietor's funds, Net profit Ratio and Gross profit Ratio. So L.IC Must try to Increase Profit.

Here Rank- 1 indicate the good condition of Rank-2,

We see in table No- 4.10, Standard Deviation of E.P.S is 1707.156 so it gives a Rank-1, Standard Deviation of Return on Capital Employed is 16.868 so it take rank -2, Standard Deviation of Operating Expenses is 12.8152 so it take Rank-3, Standard Deviation of Return on Proprietor's Funds is 2.93014 so it take Rank – 4, Standard Deviation of Gross Profit is 0.61062 so it take Rank- 5 and at last Standard Deviation of Net Profit Ratio is 0.594 so it take Rank – 6.

Above ranking we conclude that Earning per share is higher than Return on capital Employed, Operating expenses, Return on Proprietor's funds, Gross profit Ratio and Net profit Ratio. So L.IC Must try to Increase Profit.

Here we gives a lowest coefficient of variation Rank-1 to Highest is last.

We see in table No-4.10, Coefficient of Variation of Operating expenses is 6.904716 so it gives a Rank-1, Coefficient of Variation of Net Profit is 8.897097 so it take rank -2, Coefficient of Variation Gross Profit is 9.64163 of so it take Rank-3, Coefficient of Variation of Return on Proprietor's Funds is 12.44111 so it take Rank – 4, Coefficient of Variation of Earning Per share is 19.37746 so it take Rank – 5, Coefficient of Variation of Return on Capital Employed is 33.3342 so it take Rank – 6

Above ranking we conclude that operating expenses is higher than Net profit, Gross profit, Return on Proprietor's funds, Earning Per share and return on Capital Employed . So L.IC Must try to Increase Profit.

Mean of current Ratio is 2.014 , Standard Deviation of Current Ratio is 0.354443 and coefficient of variation of current ratio is 17.59897. L.I.C 's Liquidity conditions is good.

Reference:

1. 'Financial management'. Ravi.m.Kishoire New Delhi Publication, July -2005

2. www.google.com

3. www.yahoo.com

4. www.capitaline.com

5. Financial management mc grew hill 1978,

6. Ohm Pakistan " Ratio analysis management in new perspective" Himalaya publication 1983

7. Maheshwari S.N." Management accounting and financial control sultan chant and sons new devil

8. Vincent marrow" handbook at financial analysis" prentice hall, Englewood new sersoy, 1989.

Chapter -5
Findings, Conclusions & Suggestions

5.1 Introduction:

For Material existence human being has three basic needs, bread(Food), Cloth and shelter(Residence) and one additional is Life Insurance.

But in the materialistic world only bread will not do enough without better cloth, just simple to cover/protect body will not do without range at selection. Residence will not do enough without luxurious facilities. Insurance will not do enough without number of life Products.

All these can be gained by not only by huge earning but availability of all these must be three which ultimately through the industrial and technological development and advancement

Many at the well established Indian industrial houses have achieved development and are the path at significant advancement of global level Reliance, Birla, Tata, Singhania, Bajaj, L.I.C, G.IC are few name amongst them have notably contributed to economic development.

Present study from the financial point at view is steered to as profitability. Analysis at selected Life Insurance Corporation Of India. The financial analysis can also be know at project evaluation. Obviously, it scope is very vast. The objective at this study may also become year vast. But in the present study for view point at profitability only.

the profitability form different angle have been the subject matters. Conclusion, being presented here have been drawn primarily at the basis of profitability analysis only based on annual accounts at Life Insurance Corporation of India.

In forgiven chapters we have made in attempt to examine Ratio, common size statement and trend analyze of Life Insurance Corporation Of India in this regard. This chapter summerises the important findings, conclusion of the study and offers a few suggestions for Life Insurance Corporation Of India

5.2 Major Findings

The main findings of present study are :

1. We have seen that LIC's Income shown decreased Trend.

2. We have seen that LIC's Expenses shown Increased Trend.

3. We have seen that Policyholder's Investments shown decreased Trend.

4. We have seen that Current Ratio and Earning per share shown increasing Trend.

5. We have seen that Loan was increased by 50% in terms of money but in total Assets Percentage it shown decreased Trend.

6. We have seen that Return On Capital Employed, Return On Proprietor's funds and Working Capital turn over was decreased trend as compare to research period.

7. We have seen that surplus was increasing in terms of money but Gross profit ratio shown decreasing trend.

8. We have seen that Net profit was increasing in terms of money but Net Profit ratio shown decreasing Trend.

9.   We have seen that Provision of LIC is higher.

10.   We have seen that the Operating Expenses ratio and Long term funds to Fixed Assets shown fluctuate Trend.

5.3   Conclusion

The main Conclusion of present study are:

1.   LIC's Net Profit ratio shown decreasing trend but decreasing percentage was minor point.

2.   LIC's Provision is high so LIC's Repayment Capacity was it reveals solvent situation for Policyholders.

3.   LIC's short term solvency is excellent..

4.   LIC's Earning per share capacity shown so much high. The

5.   investors must invest their money in LIC's Equity share capital.

6.   LIC's Return on Capital Employed Performance was good.

7.   LIC's Return on Proprietor's Funds shown near about 3 times so investor's must invest their money in LIC's Capital Funds.

8.   LIC's Working capital Turnover shown 6 times so we can say that LIC's more utilize their working capital under research period.

9.   LIC's uses policyholder's funds for purchasing Fixed Assets.

10.   As we have seen that after establishment of LIC's it's equity capital shown same till study period so we can say that LIC's gives more benefits to their old Shareholders.

5.4 Suggestions

As we find LIC is on better position, Inspite of it's better position if it will take following steps in to consideration, the chances of it's being a best company of India are more.

1.   Life Insurance Corporation Of India should take necessary steps to minimize operating expenses.

2.   L.I.C's Lending Loan was raised by 50% only so L.I.C must try to increase it.

3.   Life Insurance Corporation Of India must take necessary steps for maintain and increase current ratio like increasing current assets.

4.   For increasing Return on capital Employed, Return on proprietor's funds and Net profit. Life Insurance Corporation Of India should take necessary steps to increase income like increase sale of number of policies, increase premium rate, sale investments on high rate, reduce operating expenses and other expenses.

5.   Life Insurance Corporation Of India has invested policyholder's funds into fixed assets so L.I.C should raised their Long term funds like equity share capital, borrowings etc and avoid use of policyholder's funds.

5.5 Further research in the topic of Financial Analysis

After the analysis, interpretation and show the limitation we find the rest of the are a for further research are:

1.   A similar research can be taken in other industry like Pharmaceutical, steel, cement, textile, paper, pipe etc.,

2.   A study can be undertaken of other Life Insurance companies in India.

3.   A study can be undertaken of other Non life Insurance companies in India.

BIBLIOGRAPHY

1. REFERENCES

1. Dr. S.N. Maheswari   :- Financial Management- principles & practice – sultanchand & sons pub. 2008

2. Dr. C.R.Kothari   :- Research Methodologes,1997 New Delhi,Vishwa prakashan

3. Bharat Jhunjhunwala   :- "Business Statistics" – 2008 S.Chand & Company Ltd.

4. Ashish Bhattacharya   :- "Essentials of Financial Accounting", 2007 Prentice Hall of India pvt Ltd.

5. Kulkarni P.V   :- "Financial Management"- Himalaya Publication House. 2009

6. Dr. R.S Patel.,   :- "Statistical Methods for Educational Research" Jay Publication 2010,

7. Kulshreshtha N.K   :- "Analysis of Financial Statements Of Paper Industry in India" 2010 Navman Prkashan New Delhi

8. N.P. Agrawal   :- "Issues In Financial Management" 2007 - RBSA Publishers New Delhi

9. Dr. S.J Parmar :- "Financial Efficiency" 2008

Raj Publishers

10. P.C. Tulsian :- "Financial Accounting" 2010
Bharat Publication, Ahmedabad

11. S. Balachandran :- IC-33 Life Insurance (New syllabus)
2010, Insurance Institute Of India

2. Magazine/News paper

1. The Times Of India

2. Life Insurance In India – New Delhi

3. The Financial Express

4. The Economic Times

5. The Indian Express

3. website

1. http:// www.google.com //

2. http://www.lic.com//

3. http://www.irda.com//

4. http://www.capitaline.com//

4. Journal

1. The Analyst

2. Indian Journal of Marketing

3. The management accountant

4. Applied Finance

Annual Reports of Life Insurance Corporation Of India
Revenue Account (Rs.,000)

particulars	2006	2007	2008	2009	2010
Net Premium	907591972	1277822594	149705581	1571865504	1859859122
Income From Investments (a) Interest, dividend and rent-Gross	354786372	405724002	479987892	400000000	671978843
(b) Profit on sale of Investments	45677646	51099897	83751700	27757255	451972144
other Income	13412841	9601080	2834339	3183766	3405342
Total	1321468831	1744247573	2063629812	2002806525	2987215451
Commission	70949194	91690668	95680966	100332433	121103128
Operating Expenses	60415606	70858411	83093206	90642874	122458242
Provision for Doubtful Debts	2097558	4116661	1356845	2731058	--
Other expenses - Exchange	511028	--	416694	190944	1225618
Provision for Taxation	39677545	46658157	35104569	33484805	36252874
Provision other than Taxation	403646	638235	1579138	9317688	5045539
Benefits paid	339271106	532864555	565503261	524781387	791306584
Bonuses Paid	2972382	13957115	10730870	7722299	10035393
changes in valuation of liability in respect of life policies	692662266	739433939	895564018	1077704876	1161786538
Transfer to provision for linked Liabilities	106290795	236451743	366304348	146607003	727473877
Transfer to fund for future appropriation	-	-	-	-	218431
Surplus - Transfer to P & L A/c	6217705	7578089	8295897	9291158	10309227
Total	1321468831	1744247573	2063629812	2002806525	2987215451

Profit & Loss Account (Rs.,000)

Particulars	2006	2007	2008	2009	2010
Surplus - Transfer From Revenue A/c	6217705	7578089	8295897	9291158	10309227
Income from Investments Interest, Dividends and Rent	99465	158114	155235	282330	297953
Total	6317170	7736203	8451132	9573488	10607180
Indirect Expenses	1369	0	4873	-	12
Profit	6315801	7736203	8446259	9573488	10607168
Total	6317170	7736203	8451132	9573488	10607180

Balance sheet (Rs.,000)

Particulars	2006	2007	2008	2009	2010
Source of funds					
Shareholder's funds	1769985	2928099	3078461	3360791	3658732
policyholder's funds	5311861171	6256641789	7765970917	8408774765	11169691480
funds for future appropriations	272373	-	-	593136	811567
current Liabilities	213075592	202667136	220878503	195902190	219021982
Total	552697121	6462237024	7989927881	8608630882	11393183561
Application of funds					
Investments Shareholder's	1664043	2794518	2931963	3195040	3537627
Policyholder's	4527864215	5111128330	6053970106	6389617039	8330412670
Assets held to cover linked Liabilities	123152814	360305983	751762963	904102929	1703251763
Loans	551243796	630815240	732135620	794771155	829970874
Fixed Assets	12621446	14035573	21176952	29798044	31229886
current Assets cash and bank balances	128020227	132980698	177397693	172926356	141589291
advances and other assets	182412580	210176682	250552584	314220319	353191650
Total	5526979121	6462237024	7989927881	8608630882	11393183561